D0802471

Eccentric
COLORADO

Eccentric COLORADO

A LEGACY OF THE BIZARRE AND UNUSUAL

BY
KENNETH JESSEN

PRUETT **P** PUBLISHING COMPANY
Boulder, Colorado

First Edition
1 2 3 4 5 6 7 8 9

Printed in the United States of America

Library of Congress Cataloging In Publication Data

Jessen, Kenneth Christian.
  Eccentric Colorado.

  Bibliography: p.
  Includes index.
  1. Colorado—History—Miscellanea. I. Title.
F776.6.J47 1985   978.8   85-500
ISBN 0-87108-682-4 (pbk.)

Cover photos courtesy of the Denver Public Library

To my wonderful sons,
Todd, Chris, and Ben

Acknowledgments

The idea for this book came from Lee Gregory, author of *Colorado Scenic Guide* (in two volumes, one for the northern region and one for the southern region; Johnson Publishing Co.). Lee also supplied ideas throughout this project, then acted as an editor. Rand Marshall, using his journalism background, edited the manuscript to improve its readability. Special thanks goes to Merilee Eggleston at Pruett Publishing Co. for her excellent job of final editing. Help in the area of photographs came from Eleanor Gehres and Augie Mastrogiuseppe at the Denver Public Library's Western History Department and from Collette C. Chambellan at the Colorado Historical Society. Most of the research was done at the Loveland Public Library, and my thanks goes to their staff. My dear wife, Sonje, also had to put up with many late nights while I wrote this work.

This book was made possible by all of those wonderful Colorado characters like Soapy Smith, Alferd Packer, John O'Keefe, and Nikola Tesla.

Kenneth Jessen
Loveland, Colorado 1985

Contents

Introduction

During its development, Colorado's economy was based
primarily on the extraction of gold, silver, and other metals.
Would-be miners and prospectors poured into the territory,
and by the 1870s the Colorado mountains were filled with
hundreds of shanty towns. Along with the miners came
promoters and investors. Other less desirable people were
also attracted to Colorado. Countless transients, down on their
luck or broken by the Civil War, entered the state to try to
find their own bonanza. Society was highly mobile, with
residents of any given mining town owing their loyalty to it
only so long as the mines continued to produce. As a network
of railroads was constructed, even some of the presumably
more stable towns based on agriculture were abandoned if
bypassed by the twin bands of steel.

The environment in Colorado provided a fertile setting for
some great con games, hoaxes, and legends. The combination
of hard living and severe mountain weather led to bizarre
behavior, including cannibalism. Old legends were em-
bellished upon and perpetuated, while others were created.
But the arrival of the twentieth century and of modern times
did not entirely stem the tide of unusual events. Colorado
remains a place to find the unexpected.

This collection of hoaxes, legends, and tales of eccentricity
is derived primarily from accounts written at the time and
are to be enjoyed for what they are. They were selected
because they captured the imagination of this author.

Kenneth Jessen
Loveland, Colorado 1985

*Colorado's
Diamond Field*

The history of Colorado is filled with stories of thousands of men walking and riding horseback through virgin forests, crossing crystal clear mountain streams, poking into every cranny of exposed rock, and searching for quick riches. The state had not been fully explored by the 1870s, and was still full of mystery in the minds of those willing to endure many hardships. The men attracted to the frontier were not above any means of making a quick dollar. Practically every visitor to the state was looking for a pot of gold, and it didn't take long before some of them capitalized on the excessive greed of others.

A pair of dirty, bearded, disheveled prospectors came to San Francisco one foggy morning in 1872. Philip Arnold and John Slack looked like they had run out of luck as they waited near the front door of a prominent bank. When the first employee arrived, they asked to be let in. The pair looked up and down the street and were wary of anyone who might be watching. Once inside, Arnold cautiously pulled out a small leather pouch. The two men asked the employee if it could be kept in the bank's vault. The employee was curious about the pouch's contents and asked what it contained. Arnold and his partner scanned the bank's empty lobby as if to seek out someone in hiding. The employee swore he would never tell another soul about the pouch. The prospectors poured the contents on a table, and much to the amazement of the employee, the pouch contained raw diamonds.

Philip Arnold and John Slack vanished into the San Francisco fog and remained out of sight for several weeks. They counted on human nature, and sure enough, the employee showed the sack full of diamonds to the bank's officers. They, in turn, contacted some wealthy investors. A frantic search was made for the prospectors. Arnold and Slack came out of hiding and, at first, resisted any offers to let others in on the location of their diamond field. Finally, they reluctantly agreed to be a part of a new company called the New York and San Francisco Mining and Commercial Company. Their newfound colleagues paid them $600,000 (more than $6 million in today's dollars) to be let in on the secret discovery. Tiffany and Company in New York City appraised the gems and informed the investors of their great value.

One of California's best-known geologists, Henry Janin, was hired as a consultant to inspect the newly discovered diamond field. Arnold and Slack swore Janin to secrecy and took him to their find. Janin proclaimed the diamond field to be genuine. The diamond hoax was working perfectly.

News of the discovery leaked to the newspapers. To keep rumors of the diamond field alive, the prospectors appeared in Laramie, Denver, and Salt Lake City during 1872. They showed their precious stones, and the newspapers spread the latest information far and wide.

Speculation held that the diamond field was located in northeastern Arizona, or in New Mexico, or possibly in the San Luis Valley of Colorado. Had the purported diamond field been in any of these locations, it would have been of little interest to Clarence King and his team of government geologists. But one rumor held the location to be inside the boundaries of the Fortieth Parallel Survey that King and his associates had just spent six years working to complete. The survey was an effort to discover what was in the one-hundred-mile-wide land grant for the Union Pacific and Central Pacific railroads. Not a single precious stone had been discovered, nor had the members of the survey team found a geologic formation in which gems were likely to occur. But if they had overlooked a diamond field, their professional reputations would be on the line. Before King could issue the final report on the Fortieth Parallel Survey, he had to determine the validity of the discovery.

Samuel Emmons and fellow geologist James Gardner were part of King's team. On October 5, 1872, the pair took a westbound train from Battle Mountain, Nevada, where they had been doing field work. At first, they paid little attention to their fellow passengers, but at breakfast the following morning, they noticed a group of men in rough clothes. Their tan faces gave them away as returning from some type of outdoor work. By sheer coincidence, Emmons and Gardner had boarded a train with surveyors returning from the diamond field.

Fellow geologist Henry Janin was in the party. Emmons and Gardner questioned him and learned that he had been unable to visit the claim because he was being followed. The rest of the party took such a roundabout route they became lost. Once at the diamond field, the men were given one hour to look for jewels using only their pocket knives. The ten surveyors returned with 280 diamonds and many rubies. The stones ranged in size from a pea to a small grain. Janin did not, however, give the slightest clue as to where the diamond field was located.

Clarence King quickly gathered a small team of government geologists to investigate the alleged diamond field. He determined that the Janin party had left the Union Pacific between Green River and Rawlins. A general description of the area where the diamonds were located was extracted from one of the members of the Janin party.

Armed with a meager amount of information, the government geologists set out to find the diamond field. They reasoned that the location was south of the railroad, at the base of a peak, and about ten miles north of Brown's Park, placing it just south of the Colorado-Wyoming line. In October of 1872, the King party, including Emmons and Gardner, left San Francisco. To avoid suspicion, their code word for diamonds was "carboniferous fossils." After their arrival at Fort Bridger, Wyoming, the officers and soldiers at the fort weren't very surprised that the team was after "carboniferous fossils." And just as they were leaving on horseback, the post surgeon whispered into Emmon's ear, "Bring me back a couple of solitaires, will you?" It was simply hard to keep the expedition a secret.

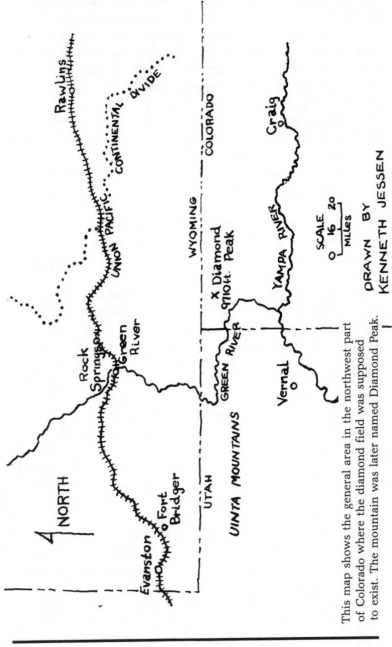

This map shows the general area in the northwest part
of Colorado where the diamond field was supposed
to exist. The mountain was later named Diamond Peak.

The weather was bitterly cold, with temperatures driven below zero by a relentless wind. The bleak, treeless expanse of prairie offered no protection or relief from the elements. The animals were worn out, and their legs became encased in balls of ice from crossing the streams. After four days, the party crossed the Green River. Finally, one of the men found a written claim signed by Henry Janin. This led them to a table rock area, and the men were encouraged by the discovery of a few diamonds and rubies. It was late in the day on November 2, 1872, and Emmons wrote in his diary, "That night we were full-believers in the verity of Janin's reports, and dreamed of the untold wealth that might be gathered."

The following morning the men came to a startling conclusion: the number of gems decreased rapidly outside the windswept table rock at the center of the claim. The frequency of occurrence was studied. There were always about one dozen rubies for every diamond found. Nature certainly doesn't maintain a ratio of precious stones. By using their sieves, the men were only able to find gems where the earth had been disturbed. Nothing more than common quartz crystals were found where the soil was untouched. The anthills gave yet another clue that the area had been salted. Some of the hills had a footprint close by and small holes had been made near the entrance produced by the ants. At the bottom of each hole, a ruby or two could be recovered, but on any other place on the hill, there were no gem stones. Anthills with no footprints yielded no gemstones.

In King's party was a middle-aged German. He was not wealthy and had never been in a place where diamonds could be simply picked up. He didn't want to leave despite the intense cold and constant wind. While he was washing dirt and occasionally pocketing a sparkler, he came across a stone that caught his eye. It filled him with wonderment since it bore the marks of the lapidary's art. He immediately called out, "Look here, Mr. King. This is the bulliest diamond field as never vas. It not only produces diamonds, but cuts them moreover also." King snatched the stone from the German's hand and everything was as clear as day; the area was salted. King hunted for more evidence and soon had proof that wholesale fraud had been committed.

A problem faced King. If he accused the prospectors of fraud when there was no fraud, his entire Fortieth Parallel Survey would be discredited and six years of hard work would go down the drain. Henry Janin had publicly pronounced the diamond field to be real and his reputation as a geologist was without fault. King elected to stay in the cold and wind to gather more evidence.

On the fourth day, a hole three feet wide and ten feet deep was dug. All of the dirt was examined, and no gems were found below the surface. The results were conclusive. King released his men, returned to San Francisco, and exposed the diamond hoax. He saved many small, potential investors from losing money, and he may have saved the lives of prospectors trying to endure the winter by hunting gems in this remote part of Colorado. King was heralded as a hero and as a credit to the government survey team.

The trustees of the San Francisco and New York Mining and Commerical Company selected an investigating committee to ferret out and punish those guilty of the fraud. Everyone connected with the early history of the diamond field was sought. An accomplice of Arnold and Slack by the name of Cooper stepped forward. He admitted with noble candor that he was the author of the entire scheme. He felt he was unrightfully deprived by his welching partners of his just share of the spoils. Salting gold and silver mines was nothing new and had been overworked. Cooper suggested to Arnold and Slack that salting a diamond field would be a pleasing variation. He told them that small industrial grade diamonds could be used for the task. Once the fraud was under way, Cooper was excluded from the details. His confession was motivated by revenge and was given first to the investigating committee, then to a grand jury in San Francisco.

The diamonds and other gems were purchased in bulk from

dealers in London and Amsterdam. One dealer even identified a photograph of Arnold. Using $35,000 raised through the sale of some mining property, Arnold and Slack invested in industrial gemstones of the lowest quality. From that investment, a profit (after expenses) of $600,000 was reaped from the salted Colorado diamond field.

Once Arnold received his booty from the San Francisco and New York Mining and Commercial Company, he retired to his home in Elizbethtown in Hardin County, Kentucky. He purchased some fine property and had a safe installed in his home. He was surrounded by a host of relatives and friends.

After the fraud was uncovered by King, attorneys were hired to recover the money. A suit for $350,000 was brought against Arnold. He then publicly denied the charges in the Louisville *Journal* on December 20, 1872. Arnold, however, admitted his safe contained $550,000 which he said was the result of arduous labor as a prospector and miner. He was outraged that men from California were trying to take his wealth and to connect him with fraud. Arnold was quite clever and quoted Janin's report and the appraisal from Tiffany. He claimed he turned over a good diamond field to the investors and if any salting had been done, it took place later.

Hardin County applauded Arnold's spunk for sticking up for his rights and for standing his ground unflichingly against outside intruders. Eventually, the lawyers became convinced that not a dollar could be wrung from Arnold no matter what proof was submitted in court. From a political and legal standpoint, Arnold lived in an impenetrable fortress. To gain immunity from any further litigation, Arnold surrendered $150,000.

The way was now paved for Arnold to live out his life in luxury, but he wanted to enter the world of finance. He opened a bank in Elizabethtown and did a good business based on his popularity. He loaned a rival bank $8,000, and when the collateral for this loan was not surrendered on time, Arnold brought suit. An officer of the bank, Harry Holdsworth, made some derogatory comments in a letter about Arnold's character. One thing led to another, and on a street in Elizabethtown, August 14, 1878, Arnold attacked Holdsworth with a cane, striking him a good number of solid blows.

The next day Arnold was drinking beer in Lott's Saloon when Holdsworth walked in. Arnold threw him to the floor and hit him with his fists. Holdsworth was so bloody he could not see, and he begged Arnold to stop. Only after a law officer interceded did Arnold stop his attack.

After getting cleaned up, Holdsworth went back to his bank and got a double-barreled, sawed-off shotgun. He marched back to Lott's Saloon with the weapon in the crook of his arm. Arnold was standing in front of the building, and when he saw Holdsworth, he drew his pistol and fired two shots. Both shots missed, but so did Holdsworth's first load of buckshot. Holdsworth took cover behind a tree as Arnold advanced down the street. The second discharge from the shotgun, delivered at only two feet, badly lacerated Arnold's shoulder. Holdsworth dropped his weapon and ran for his life in a hail of bullets from Arnold's gun. All of Arnold's shots missed, but a local farmer was seriously wounded by a stray round.

In February of 1879, Philip Arnold caught pneumonia and died. His wound had healed, but remained painful. Many felt that the wound weakened him and brought on the pneumonia.

As for John Slack, every effort was made to track him down. Arnold had all or almost all of the money. Slack could not have received much over $30,000. It was assumed that the two men must have planned a fifty-fifty split. Maybe Arnold died before Slack could collect his share. Slack lived out his life as a coffin maker first in St. Louis then in White Oaks, New Mexico. He died at the age of seventy-six.

From left to right: James T. Gardner, Richard D. Cotter, William H. Brewer, and Clarence King. All were members of the Fortieth Parallel Survey and were surprised when it leaked out that diamonds had been discovered in an area they had studied carefully. King was instrumental in uncovering the hoax partially to save his credibility as a geologist.

(United States Geological Survey)

Legend of the Great Sand Dunes

The scientific explanation of why the Great Sand Dunes are located at the base of the Sangre de Cristo Mountains is quite simple. The arid floor of the San Luis Valley is sparsely covered with vegetation. The prevailing winds blow from the southwest across the valley picking up loose grains of sand. The grains bounce across the valley floor toward the Sangre de Cristos. The mountains form a 6,000-foot high barrier with the exception of the area north of Blanca Peak where Music, Medano, and Mosca passes are located. The wind is funneled into this low point, and as it rises over the mountains, it loses much of its energy. The sand ceases its movement across the valley floor and comes to rest, forming the Great Sand Dunes.

The dunes are quite strange. They rise over 700 feet above their surroundings and extend for ten miles along the base of the mountains. The dunes press into the forest and look entirely out of place. The wind causes the sand to constantly shift against the fixed backdrop of the rugged Sangre de Cristos. Flowing along the edge of the dunes is Medano Creek. Water flows over its bed of sand in pulsations called bores.

Long before a scientific explanation for the dunes existed, however, mankind was compelled to offer some reason for their presence. This led to a variety of legends. The earliest account of how these great dunes were formed may be the following story, which appeared in the August 6, 1885 issue of the *Alamosa Journal*.

A party of men camped near the great dunes in 1885. During dinner, a Spaniard entered the camp. As he drew near the light from the fire, the men could see that he had long, black, curly hair that fell from beneath a broad-brimmed sombrero. He had large black eyes, a narrow chin, and his mouth was partially hidden by a large black moustache. He stood over six feet tall, and the men guessed that he was around forty years old. In his hand was a Winchester rifle, and a Colt 45 revolver was stuck in his cartridge belt. As he stepped toward the fire, he greeted the men with, "Buenas tardes, señores."

The men welcomed him in Spanish and invited him to stay. He was asked if he understood English, and he said he did. He introduced himself as Francis Gonzalez. He added that he was from New Mexico, where he owned a large hacienda. The reason he came to the San Luis Valley was to hunt elk, but now he found himself twenty miles from his camp. The men asked him to spend the night.

One of the men expressed curiosity about how the great dunes of sand were formed. For a moment Gonzalez remained silent, then, gazing into the campfire, said, "Señor, if it would please you, I can relate to you how the famous sand dunes of the San Luis Valley really came into existence. There are undoubtedly many who can tell you this tale, but there is no one living who would be more apt to know the truth in regard to it than myself; for it was my grandfather who started the formation of the largest one in the range with part of his herd of sheep and several of his herders."

The eyes of the men lit up with wild enthusiasm and they begged Gonzalez to continue with his story. The Spaniard spoke.

"It's been ten years if not more since I last repeated what I am to tell you tonight, and although it may seem almost incredible to you, it is, nevertheless, true. What I am to repeat to you was told to me by my father and has been told by me to my children.

"It was the year 1816 that my grandfather, Don Louis Gonzalez, returned to his home in Mexico where he had enormous herds of cattle and sheep. He had developed his herd by making trips north into New Mexico and southern Colorado.

"He had penetrated into this part of Colorado and had traveled over the San Luis Valley. Feed was here in such abundance that my grandfather returned to his home completely charmed with this part of the world and was fully determined to brave Indians and hardships...to send a small portion of his herd of sheep, in (the) charge of some of his Mexican herders, to this valley. He, therefore, selected 3,500 sheep from his herd, picked out five of his most trusty herders, and sent them upon their journey. They traveled may hundred leagues, and it was in the springtime that they arrived at their destination.

"They immediately set (to) work building cabins to live in and corrals for the sheep. A month had passed away and the sheep were thriving wonderfully, and nothing had occurred to give them warning of their approaching doom.

"On the twenty-fifth of June, one herder, Martinez by name, proposed to go over the mountains and see what kind of country lay on the other side. He started out during the fairest of weather and passed through Mosca Pass. After three days spent in wandering around the eastern side of the range he started to return to his companions. He pursued his way through the pass with no foreboding of the horrible fate that had overtaken those left behind, and at last arrived at the mouth of the pass.

"He looked, and where he should have seen the newly erected cabins and the herd peacefully grazing, he saw only an immense mountain of sand. He was dumbfounded and could not believe (it) at first...or else he had lost his way and his companions, with the sheep, were off in some other direction. After going a short distance farther and seeing many familiar landmarks, he at last came to realize what had happened: Where now stood only a large hill of sand was where his home had been for the last month.

"He started immediately to find his brother herders, but after searching for them for two days he gave them up as lost. A storm had risen during his absence and buried the 3,500 sheep, his four companions, their houses, and corrals beneath fifty feet of sand. That was the beginning of the famous sand dunes of Colorado. The herder who had escaped the fate of his companions then set out to carry the news to my grandfather, and after encountering many hardships, he at last arrived at the hacienda and related to his master all he knew.

"Sand storms year after year have kept piling the sand in this heap until, today, it stands fully 800 feet high above the bones of those who perished there. . .years ago.

"Hill after hill was formed from that, until now there exists a chain extending many miles up the valley. A search was made for the bodies of the Mexicans who perished there, but before laborers could succeed in getting ten feet below the surface, the excavation made would completely fill with the loose sand, and the undertaking was abandoned."

After Señor Gonzalez finished his tale of how the great sand dunes were started, he rolled himself up in his blanket and fell fast asleep, leaving his companions to ponder the truth about the mysterious, ever-shifting sand dunes.

Medano Creek flows along the base of the Great Sand Dunes. Its water flows over a bed of sand in pulsations called bores. This is just one of the strange features of the dunes, which rise over 700 feet above the valley floor and extend for ten miles. *(Kenneth Jessen)*

Quickstep Regains His Job

*A*t just a nickel a trip, the Cherrelyn horsedrawn car was was a popular weekend excursion. The four-wheeled railcar carried passengers from the foot of the hill on South Broadway in Englewood to its top at Cherrelyn Village. After the horse and car reached the top of the hill, the animal was unhitched and allowed to climb up the steps onto the rear platform. The car was then given a push by John Bogue, the driver, conductor, and lessee, and the vehicle would coast slowly down the gentle grade. About halfway down, the grade increased and the car would pick up speed. During the summer, the car would stop on a small wooden trestle to allow a commercial photographer to snap a photo of the horse, car, and people hanging out of the windows. On sunny days the horse would sport a straw hat. Passengers enjoyed the ride so much that the horse-powered car remained in service from 1892 to 1910. The line was jokingly referred to as the Gravity & Bronco street railroad.

On January 7, 1900, a strong wind began to blow which materially interfered with the normal operation of the horse-gravity railroad. During the descent, when the car reached a shallow portion of the grade, the wind brought the car to a complete stop. John Bogue did not have the heart to ask his horse, Quickstep, to get off and pull. Instead he called upon his passengers to push the car until the grade became steeper.

At the base of the hill on this particular day, Bogue noticed an unusual number of potential passengers waiting to ride. Also, the velocity of the wind had increased. The situation called for some creative thinking, so John rose to the occasion. For years, Quickstep had been the sole motive power for the car and had hauled it up the hill and had ridden back down countless times. Breaking with tradition, a change was introduced into the locomotion, causing the old horse's importance to dwindle.

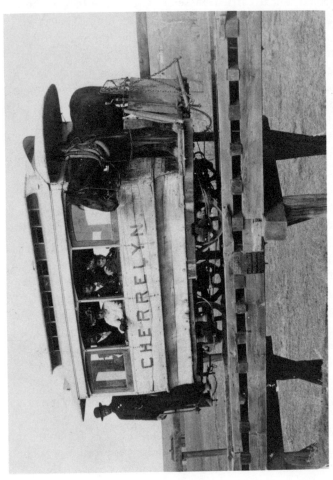

For a nickel a trip, one could ride the Cherrelyn horsedrawn car in Englewood. On the return trip down the hill from Cherrelyn Village, the horse rode on the rear platform. One particular horse, Quickstep, was the motive power for many years. *(Denver Public Library)*

John Bogue owned other horses, and one of them was pressed into service. The new arrival's duty was to help Quickstep up the hill with the fully loaded car. Where the hill leveled off, the new horse was to wait to help get the car back down the hill against the wind, with Quickstep walking behind to act as a brake if needed.

The innovation worked quite well for the first trip. On the second journey up the hill, disaster struck the entire system, resulting in a suspension of business for the rest of the day. In one place the road ran through a narrow cut, having just enough room for the horses. The sly Quickstep held to the middle of the track and successfully elbowed his new partner up the steep side of the cut. Following was the sound of a heavy fall, and the car came to a sudden stop as it derailed. The people in the car were jarred off their seats and quickly abandoned the vehicle in favor of firm ground.

The new horse had stumbled and fallen. Quickstep, as if in malicious mischief, whinnied and pulled the car over the squirming body of his fallen companion. The new horse was pinned under the front platform, and somehow his two hind legs became tangled in the metal spokes of the car wheels.

It took Bogue nearly two hours to extract the unfortunate bronco from his dangerous position. Quickstep pulled the now empty car the rest of the way up to Cherrelyn. As people learned of the accident they offered advice and sympathy. In response, Bogue delivered a short speech.

"Boys, it's my first accident and you bet your life I'll never again use a second horse, no matter how hard the wind blows. Old Quickstep will never have to quit the platform again, either, on the back trip."

Miner's Companion Is His Violin

*H*igh above the mining town of Silver Plume, a rich vein of ore was discovered in the late 1860s by Clifford Griffin. This young Englishman was one of the first miners to come to the Silver Plume area. Little was known about him except that his fiancee had been found dead the eve of their wedding. Griffin came to the Rocky Mountains to enter the mining business and to forget his sad past.

Griffin discovered a rich vein of ore and named his mine the Seven-thirty. It contained both silver and gold. The deeper the mine was developed, the richer the ore. The young Englishman soon became the wealthiest mine owner in the area. Nothing, however, caused him to forget his fiancee's untimely death, and he withdrew socially from the other miners and their families.

On the side of the steep mountain near his mine, Griffin constructed a simple cabin. His sole companion was his violin, and after the end of a day's work, he would stand at the front of his cabin and play. The sad music would drift down into Silver Plume, and miners and their families would come outside and look up to see the lonely musician by his cabin. Sometimes one of the miners would request a special tune. After he completed his mountainside recital, the miners would applaud with the sound echoing off the canyon walls.

Directly in front of his cabin, Griffin dug a grave in the solid rock. One spring evening in 1887, he played especially well. The miners applauded, then watched him walk toward the grave. Suddenly, the sharp report of a gun reverberated through the hills. Clifford Griffin was found face down in his own grave with a bullet through the heart.

In his cabin was a note requesting that he be left in the stone grave. The miners not only followed his last instructions but erected a granite marker over the grave with the following inscription:

Clifford Griffin
Son of Alfred Griffin Esq. of
Brand Hull, Shropshire, England
Born July 2, 1847
Died June 19, 1887
and in Consideration of His Own Request Buried Here

This marker can still be seen today high above Silver
Plume.

High above Silver Plume this impressive granite shaft marks the grave of Clifford Griffin. After playing a sad song on his violin, Griffin shot himself and fell into his own grave.

(Kenneth Jessen)

The Kidnapping Of Judge Stone

William Austin Hamilton Loveland, one of the great builders of Colorado, was born May 30, 1826, in Chatham, Massachusetts. He was the son of a Methodist minister. After his family moved to Illinois, William attended public schools and spent a brief period in a local college. His restlessness led him to enlist in the Mexican War as a wagon master. At Chapultepec he was severely wounded; and in 1848 he returned home to Illinois.

The following year, William Loveland traveled west in an ox-drawn wagon across the great prairie. He stopped at Grass Valley, California (between Reno and Sacramento), along with other gold seekers in the great rush of '49. He failed to find the riches of his dreams and returned home to become a merchant. In 1858, Loveland was drawn westward again by tales of gold in Colorado Territory at the base of the Rocky Mountains. After spending time at a tent camp near the mouth of Clear Creek Canyon, Loveland became interested in the supply problems of miners headed into the foothills. Later that year, Loveland and a dozen other men founded the town of Golden. After constructing the first permanent home in Golden, he set about selling supplies to miners as they passed on their way to places like Central City, Russell Gulch, and Black Hawk.

Loveland opened the first store in Golden, but he is best remembered for his recognition of transportation needs in Colorado. He founded the Colorado Central Railroad Company and built narrow gauge branches up Clear Creek Canyon to Georgetown and to Central City. A standard gauge branch was constructed from Golden to Denver, and the main line ran from Golden through Longmont, Berthoud, Loveland, and Fort Collins to Cheyenne.

When Loveland chartered his Colorado Central, it made Denver businessmen a little uneasy. From 1862 to 1867, Golden was the territorial capital of Colorado. Having the

W.A.H. Loveland, one of Colorado's pioneer railroad builders, founded the Colorado Central, which served the mining area west of Denver as well as Front Range towns north to Cheyenne. Loveland had to pull off some shady deals, however, to keep control of his line.

(Loveland Museum and Gallery)

capital in a smaller town must have been humiliating to
Denverites, and besides, it gave Golden a lot of prestige.
Loveland's general idea was to make Golden the transportation center of the Rocky Mountain region with railroads
radiating in all directions.

The Union Pacific, using the great wealth it had accumu-
lated during construction of the transcontinental line across
Wyoming, dominated Western transportation. Under the
direction of Jay Gould, the Union Pacific was not to be
denied any opportunity to expand its power and viewed
Loveland's Colorado Central as a valuable feeder line.
Although William Loveland raised some money to build his
railroad through the sale of county bonds, it was not enough.
The Union Pacific contributed large sums to the Central and
donated rails, man power, locomotives, and cars. Loveland,
however, failed to reciprocate by giving the U.P. any control
over how the money was spent. As a result, Jay Gould plotted
to gain control over the Colorado Central by forcing it into
receivership and then consolidating it with two other railroads.

Since the consolidation scheme would have sacrificed
local control of the Colorado Central, the county's residents
supported Loveland's efforts to resist the U.P. In May of 1876,
Loveland's forces, having been denied the legal right to take
charge of the road, took it physically. On May 21, Loveland,
his superintendent, assistant superintendent, and Secretary
E.L. Berthoud walked to the Golden depot and began relieving
the Union Pacific men of their duties. They continued
to the shops, freight house, and roundhouse replacing
the men with Colorado Central employees. As a narrow
gauge train pulled into the Golden yards, its crew was also
replaced, and so on until Loveland controlled the entire
railroad. The Central employees slept with their guns. Some
track was torn up and telegraph lines were cut, presumably
by U.P. men, but repairs were made quickly and train
schedules were maintained.

The Union Pacific filed an injunction against the Colorado
Central, but it was ignored. On August 12, 1876, the Union

Pacific went to court in Boulder and forced the Central into receivership to cover a million and a half dollars for material, rolling stock, locomotives, and so on: all furnished by the Union Pacific to make the Central operational. David H. Moffat, Jr. was tentatively appointed by Judge A.W. Stone as receiver for the properties of the Colorado Central.

This led to an unusual sequence of events in the history of Colorado railroads. Loveland and the counties holding stock in the Central were determined to keep the Union Pacific from gaining control. The Central's board of directors met in special session with their lawyers. After taking the matter under advisement, the lawyers concluded the Central must either pay interest on its indebtedness to the U.P. or prevent Judge Stone from reaching Boulder on August 15 to conclude transfer of the railroad to the receiver.

The board of directors got in touch with Mott Johnson, a 59'er who later became sheriff of Jefferson County. Mott was asked to organize a band of men to stop the train from Denver, remove Judge Stone, and hold him captive until the term of the court expired on August 16. Mott contacted his close friend Carlos Lake who helped him organize and lead the band of men. About twenty men were invited to a secret meeting, but six, a little leery of these shenanigans, were excused.

At 2:00 the morning of August 15, 1876, a band of armed men on horseback gathered in Golden. One horseman brought an extra mount for the judge and another arrived in a light carriage. A party was sent to Denver to telegraph Golden and determine if the judge had boarded the morning train, and a second party positioned themselves at the Golden depot to intercept the telegram. One member with a fast horse was to ride to the ambush point and alert the band if the judge was on the train.

The group of riders headed for the point were the Colorado Central crossed Ralston Creek. They piled ties high on the track and remained hidden waiting for the train to pass through around 9:00 A.M. About fifteen minutes before the train was to arrive, the messenger from Golden rode his lathered horse to the ambush point and told the men that the judge was on board. The men scattered to both sides of the track when they heard the mournful wail of the approaching train. They all tied masks over their faces and got out their guns.

The engineer sighted the barricade of ties and also saw someone attempting to flag down the train. As the locomotive came to a halt, masked gunmen appeared and kept the frightened engineer and fireman covered. Carlos Lake and a husky young German immigrant entered the coach and singled out Judge Stone. A .45 caliber "equalizer" was used to convince the judge that he best leave the train quickly. The judge was placed in the carriage and whisked off toward the foothills.

After hearing of the kidnapping, W.A.H. Loveland added a certain irony to this whole affair by telegraphing Governor John L. Routt asking for permission to organize a posse to arrest these men and recover the judge. Routt's answer was, "Have your sheriff procure a writ for the kidnappers. He is authorized by law to summon (a) posse large enough to execute (the) writ if it takes every man in your county or state."

Governor Routt was absolutely furious over the events and immediately extended the term of the court. He assigned Judge Brazee to take Judge Stone's place for the Boulder hearing. That afternoon, a special train ran to Boulder carrying Judge Brazee, a miliary escort, and a brass cannon on a flatcar. The court was opened at 10:00 P.M.

When Carlos Lake and the masked band of men arrived with Judge Stone at the mouth of Coal Creek Canyon, the carriage was sent back to Golden. The judge was asked to get on the extra horse, but he pleaded with the men saying that he didn't know how to ride. Lake assured him that he would be safe and that one of the men would lead the horse.

The group crossed over the ridge into the Ralston Creek drainage where they stayed most of the day. Lookouts with field glasses were posted on the ridge. In the distance they could see the tracks of the Colorado Central and take note of

Judge A.W. Stone was kidnapped on August 16, 1876 by a band of masked men to prevent him from reaching Boulder. Judge Stone was on his way to finalize the transfer of the Colorado Central Railroad to a receiver. This would have allowed the Union Pacific to gain control over the railroad.

(Colorado Historical Society)

the special train with its brass cannon. At dusk the judge was taken to a ranch owned by one of the railroad's directors. Judge Stone was treated with the greatest respect, fed a good meal, and waited on hand and foot. Later that evening, he was escorted to Golden, placed in a carriage, and returned to Denver. He was released in front of the Alvord House late that night or possibly early the next morning.

Later, at a grand jury investigation into the kidnapping, Judge Stone admitted he was unable to identify any of his abductors except the carriage driver who returned him to Denver. The driver's name was Charlie Shockley, and a subpoena was issued to bring him before the grand jury. When a deputy marshall approached Shockley in Golden, he escaped through the back door of a cigar store and hid in a grove of trees near the Coors brewery. Carlos Lake provided a horse and some money for Shockley and suggested he take a long vacation. The identity of the well-organized band of men remained a mystery for sixty years. Carlos Lake eventually told the story of Judge Stone's kidnapping at a bar association meeting in 1936.

Even after Loveland was ordered to surrender the Colorado Central to the court-appointed receiver, he refused to do so. At this time Colorado had just gained statehood, and the judicial proceedings were transferred to a higher U.S. court. The battle between Loveland and the Union Pacific seesawed back and forth. Loveland met and parried the attacks on his railroad, and eventually the U.P. capitulated.

However, there was no room in the plans of Jay Gould and his associates for a man such as Loveland. His accomplishments were ignored, and as a result of further maneuverings by Gould, Loveland was cast off from the Colorado Central. Loveland had little to show for his nearly twenty years of work developing this railroad. In 1878, he moved to Denver and purchased the *Rocky Mountain News*. At the age of only sixty-eight, William Austin Hamilton Loveland passed away.

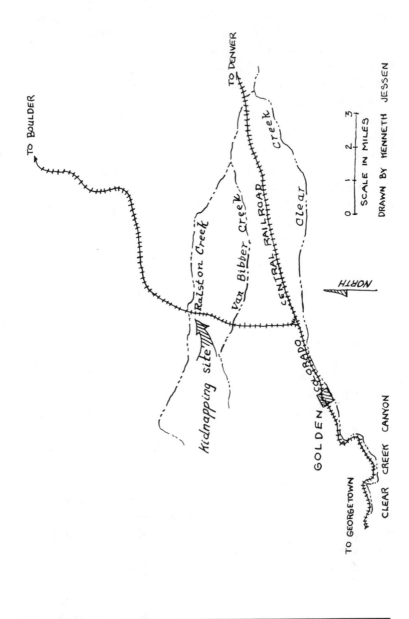

Captain Sam
Heads to the
Pacific

During the exploration of the West, it was hoped that a navigable water route could be found to the Pacific Ocean. This was an objective of Major John Wesley Powell's 1869 expedition on the Colorado River. But there were also other less well known explorers seeking a way to reach California and the Pacific Ocean by water. "Captain" Samuel Adams was one of them. He demonstrated how far a man could get on nothing but gall and the gift of gab.

Samuel Adams offered Major Powell his services. Adams claimed he had firsthand knowledge of the Colorado River. He also told Powell he was authorized by the secretary of war to explore the great river. Powell quickly sent this fast-tongued "authority" on his merry way.

In July 1869 Samuel Adams made friends with the people of Breckenridge. The small mining town was located deep in the Colorado Rockies on the Blue River. He found some individuals willing to listen and invest in a "sure thing." The plan was simple. Adams was to head up his own scientific expedition to float down the Blue River to the Colorado River and on to California and the Pacific Ocean.

His backers constructed four boats out of green lumber, the only material available in Breckenridge. The boats were open, with no decking or air compartments. Adams enlisted ten of the most able-bodied "seamen" the mining town could muster. The expedition members were equipped with muzzle-loading rifles, two hundred rounds of ammunition, and ample food supplies for the long journey. The ladies of Breckenridge made a banner for the flagship that read, "Western Colorado to California, Greetings."

It was not clear to Captain Adams just how far it was to California, that is, by water. He did know that Breckenridge was nearly two miles above sea level and that he would have to lose that distance vertically to reach the Pacific Ocean.

At the time "Captain" Samuel Adams launched his boats on the Blue
River in 1869, Breckenridge was a small, rugged mining town.
Adams promised to discover a water-level route to the Pacific Ocean,
and many of the town's residents helped finance the expedition.

(Colorado Historical Society)

There were speeches and cheers as the town gave Adams and his crew a big sendoff. Two of the four boats entered the river about two-and-a-half miles below Breckenridge, while the other two boats were hauled by wagon to a second launch area farther downstream. This strategy may have been to determine if the boats were seaworthy prior to committing all of them to the river.

During the first day, the Adams expedition traveled nine miles. The captain made observations in his ship's log as to the width and depth of the Blue River. In most instances, he left blanks for the figures he planned to fill in later. That evening, the party dined on homemade bread. Adams reported smooth sailing the first day except that his boat was upset twice.

The next day the two boats that had been sent overland arrived, and there was a new launching celebration. Judge Silverthorn made a speech and presented Captain Adams with a dog. What value the dog could have been to the expedition or even if it survived the journey remains a mystery.

On July 14, 1869 the experiences of the expedition gave its members an uncomfortable hint of what was in store for them. They swirled around a bend in the river and entered some rapids. In seconds, all but the members in the last boat were tossed into the ice cold water and were left hanging on the boulders in midstream. The "instruments" (whatever they were) and the captain's box of papers floated down the turbulent Blue.

On Sunday, July 18 one of the expedition members was sent back to Breckenridge for more "instruments" and some matches. Because of the dunking, dry matches were needed to build a fire to dry equipment and clothes. The rest of the party stayed and repaired the boats. Soon, the first signs of failing enthusiasm surfaced. Adams recorded in his diary that the party contributed $30 to a Mr. Ricker and sent him home as a "common nuisance."

Once again, expedition members pushed their boats into the Blue and continued their journey. Adams said he would go on

Captain Samuel Adams attempted to find a water route from
Breckenridge, down the Blue River, down the Colorado River, and
on to the the Pacific Ocean. For his effort, he was branded "a
preposterous, twelve-gauge, hundred-proof, kiln-dried, officially
notarized fool."

(Colorado Historical Society)

even if all others abandoned him. After a short distance, one of the boats collided with a rock and was demolished. The second set of "instruments" was lost and Adams claimed he was now at a scientific disadvantage. His entry for the day was, "Distance by water from Breckenridge, _____miles."

On the 22nd, four of the hardy explorers gave up and returned to Breckenridge. Dissension set in. The following day a party member was temporarily missing, and Adams had to man his own boat alone. He swamped it only once, and this was attributable to a fallen tree across the river. For the last eight miles to the confluence of the Blue and Colorado rivers, the water was smooth. The expedition was now fifty-five miles and twelve days from their starting point, but minus five members and one boat.

For one entire week there was a gap in the captain's diary. Possibly his pencil floated off to join his "instruments." On July 30, the party took to the water once again, and after just five miles they camped. Adams dispatched two members to Hot Sulphur Springs to bring back newspapers and more dry matches.

Farther down the Colorado River, fixed lines had to be used to keep the boats from capsizing in the swift current. Adams told the other party members that he had never seen the Colorado River so rough before. Since Adams probably had never been on the river before, he spoke the truth. One of the boats swung out of control on its line and filled with water. The party lost one hundred pounds of bacon, a sack of flour, an axe, a saw, a small oven, two canteens of salt, thirty-five pounds of coffee, and a few other items. After arriving at the bottom of this bad stretch of river, the party took stock of what provisions remained, and it wasn't much.

On August 3, they constructed paddles and used fixed lines to descend another stretch of rapids. It took an entire day to travel three hundred yards. The only good thing that happened was the recovery of a slab of bacon. They were in Gore Canyon, and as it got progressively deeper the river became a succession of rapids and waterfalls. Retreat seemed impossible.

One of the boats was swamped on August 5, and it took all morning to free it. A line attached to that same boat broke in the afternoon, and it was released to the untamed river. It disappeared beneath the foaming water. Four days of hard work were required to negotiate another three-quarters of a mile of river. In the process, nearly all of the food was lost. Only one boat remained with which to reach California.

Sam Adams may have lacked common sense and ability, but he did reason that the faster the river dropped toward the sea, the sooner he would reach smooth water. On August 6, the party threw away all extra clothing and equipment to strip down for the passage to the Pacific Ocean in one vessel. They struggled from portage to portage, but finally the boat was swamped. Its line broke, and it was dashed into the rocks by the force of the mighty Colorado River.

Captain Samuel Adams proved his dedication. He and his five companions constructed a raft and continued their journey. Finally, though, three members took a look at the pounding rapids, mused over their remaining food, and abandoned the trip. Adams and his loyal explorers packed their goods farther down the canyon. As they hiked along, they passed rocks strewn with the remains of their boats, supplies, "instruments," and clothing.

On August 10, a larger raft was built from driftwood, and the party took to the water once again. After three miles, the river delivered them straight into a boulder, dashing all hope of continuing. Adams reluctantly gave up on August 13 and set aside his quest for a water-level route to the Pacific.

Later, Sam Adams tendered a $20,000 claim to the U.S. Government for services rendered in exploring the Colorado River. All attempts to collect this and a lesser amount were rejected, since the expedition was unauthorized. History recorded that Sam Adams was "a preposterous, twelve-gauge, hundred-proof, kiln-dried, officially notarized fool, or else he was one of the most wildly incompetent scoundrels who ever lived."

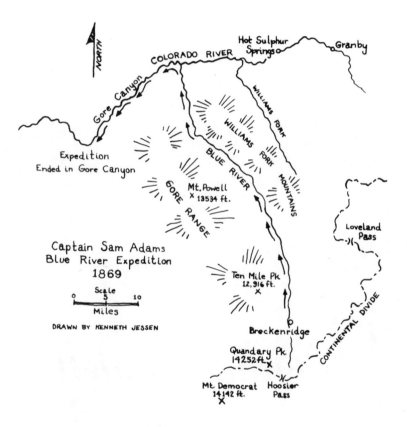

NORTH

COLORADO RIVER

Hot Sulphur Springs

Granby

Gore Canyon

Expedition
Ended in Gore Canyon

WILLIAMS FORK

WILLIAMS FORK MOUNTAINS

BLUE RIVER

GORE RANGE

Mt. Powell
X 13534 ft.

Captain Sam Adams
Blue River Expedition
1869

Scale
0   5   10
Miles

DRAWN BY KENNETH JESSEN

Ten Mile Pk.
12,916 ft.
X

Loveland
Pass

CONTINENTAL DIVIDE

Breckenridge

Quandary Pk.
14252 ft.
X

Mt. Democrat
14142 ft.
X

Hoosier
Pass

Frank Gimlett Guards The Mountains

*A*t the foot of Monarch Pass on the road from Poncha Springs was once a little town called Arbour-Villa. During the development of the mining industry in the area, Arbour-Villa was a very important place. It had the only parlor house for miles around!

The town also had a resident named Frank "Hard Rock" Gimlett. As mining dwindled and the population of Arbour-Villa declined, Frank stayed on. Eventually he was the town's only occupant. He was kept quite busy guarding the ice and snow on the high mountains and writing letters.

After looking up at the mountains for so many years, Frank became possessive of them. He thought that all this time and energy guarding them gave him the right to name them. His favorite movie star was Ginger Rogers, so he selected the name Ginger Peaks.

Gimlett began a letter writing campaign that eventually found its way to the president of the United States, who gave Gimlett an answer. He sympathized with Gimlett's campaign to name the peaks and also stated that Ginger Rogers was a fine person to name the mountains after, but renaming peaks would cause a considerable amount of inconvenience, especially among mapmakers.

Gimlett simply didn't see it that way. He let everyone know that he was not the least bit satisfied with the president's answer. In his wrath, he sat down and calculated how much the snow and ice on the mountains was worth on the open market, and how much his time was worth over all the years. Gimlett submitted a bill for $50,000 to the U.S. Government for all the years he spent guarding the snow and ice on the mountains. He also pointed out that not one shovelful had been stolen during all those years!

Frank "Hard Rock" Gimlett guarded the snow and ice on the high peaks near Monarch Pass and even tried to bill the U.S. Government for his efforts.

(Colorado Historical Society)

Depot Is
Favorite Haunt

*I*n the early days of railroading in Denver, the Denver Pacific Railroad & Telegraph Company was first to connect the town by rail to the outside world. The Denver Pacific constructed a small frame depot at 16th and Wynkoop to serve the public.

Around 1871, just a year after the Denver Pacific began service to Cheyenne, a telegraph operator named Frank Pierce removed a skull from what was then called the Rogue's Burial Ground, west of Denver. The one thing Pierce hated most of all was people spitting on the wood floor of the small depot. He took the skull and hung it on his office wall where no one could miss seeing it. A plaque was placed immediately below the skull which read, "The last man who spit upon the floor."

To separate a skull from the rest of the body, especially from a person buried in Rogue's Burial Ground, can cause all sorts of problems. As soon as the skull was placed on the depot wall to discourage would-be spitters, supernatural noises were heard during the night. The noises grew so great that the agent who succeeded Pierce had to remove the skull. He had no idea to which cemetery the skull should be returned. The ghostly knocking and thumping in the depot stopped, but the ghost remained.

A "cadaverous" figure with a shriveled, emaciated face began to prowl the area late at night around the depot. It traveled from the burial ground where its skull was exhumed and moved to Joe Bailey's old corral about twenty feet from the depot. It was seen by many people and the Denver *Times* said that the ghost, "created the wildest dismay among its observers." The railroad couldn't keep a night agent for very long. The turnover was so high that the depot was finally abandoned. In 1881, the small frame building was razed to make way for some new yard tracks and for Denver's new Union Station. The apparition ceased to haunt the area.

Colorado's
Cannibal

On November 17, 1873 a party of twenty-one miners left Salt Lake City for the newly discovered silver deposits in Colorado's San Juan Mountains. The party and its supply wagons arrived at the Ute Indian encampment at the junction of the Uncompahgre and Gunnison rivers (near the present-day town of Delta) on January 20, 1874. Ouray, chief of the Utes, advised the party not to continue into the mountains until spring because of severe weather and deep snow.

Some of the men took the advice of the wise chief and were given food by the Indians. Alferd Packer, however, was in a hurry to continue the journey and to be among the first to stake his claim. He told others in the party that he knew the country and persuaded five men to follow him. They left the Ute Indians on February 9, with provisions for ten days. Some sixty-five days later in a blinding snow storm, Packer walked into the Los Piños Indian agency (about twenty-five miles south of the present town of Gunnison). He was alone. General Adams welcomed him, and when offered breakfast, Packer turned away at the sight of food. When questioned, Alferd Packer claimed that he had traveled through the mountains subsisting on rose buds and roots. He carried a Winchester rifle but claimed it did him little good since game was scarce. He also told the general that after he became ill, his companions abandoned him. General Adams continued to question Packer about the probable fate of his companions. The vivid descriptions of his suffering in the mountains awakened the sympathy of the entire agency.

After resting for a few days, Alferd Packer went over Cochetopa Pass to Saguache, which was the nearest settlement at the time. He went on a drinking binge and spent a good deal of money in the process. He also displayed his money to others yet claimed he was penniless when he began the trip from the Ute Indian encampment.

A second party also ignored Chief Ouray's advice and headed up the Gunnison River. The first member of this party finally reached the Los Piños agency after suffering a great deal in the deep snow and cold. The man's name was Lutzenheiser, and he told General Adams that they managed to kill some game to keep from starving.

After hearing about Alferd Packer, especially how he had turned down food upon arrival at the agency, Lutzenheiser aroused the suspicions of General Adams. The feeling was that Packer probably murdered his companions and robbed them. Lutzenheiser also suspected that Packer's Winchester rifle belonged to old man Swan, a member of his party. General Adams brought Packer back to the agency to act as a guide in the hunt for his lost companions.

One of the Indians discovered what appeared to be a piece of human flesh not too far from the agency. The Indian had found it along the trail used by Packer. It was now feared that Packer not only killed his companions, but lived off of their flesh. When confronted with the evidence, Packer admitted that he was the only surviving member of his party. He claimed that the others had been killed, one after the other.

Under oath, in the presence of others from the party that traveled up the Gunnison River, Packer was forced to make a statement. He said that after running out of supplies, the party wandered for several days in the mountains. Packer left camp to gather firewood, and when he returned, old man Swan had been killed by his companions. The others were sitting around the campfire roasting his flesh. General Adams was visibly shaken by this vivid account.

After staying a day, Packer said that the remaining members of the party left the camp taking with them a supply of Swan's flesh. Humphreys died after four or five days, and they ate his flesh to stay alive. One day, Packer said, he was out again gathering firewood, and when he returned, he found Miller dead. George Noon and Wilson Bell claimed they killed him accidently, but Packer knew he had been killed

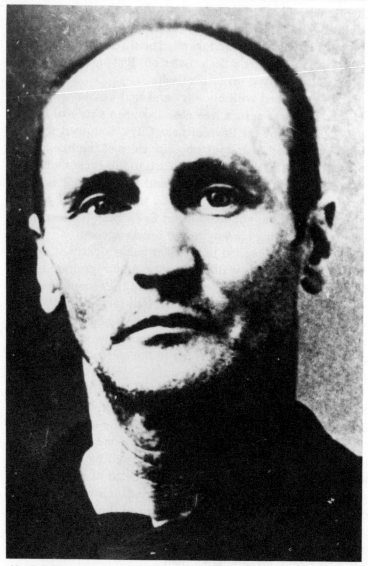

Alferd Packer was found guilty of the premeditated murder of his
five companions. His guilt has always been doubted by some, but by
his own admission, he did live on the remains of his companions
until he found his way out of the mountains.

(Colorado Historical Society)

intentionally since it had been agreed previously that Miller should be the next man sacrificed. He was a stout German, but was sick and hampered travel. The three remaining men cooked parts of Miller's flesh. Later on, Bell shot Noon, and Packer and Bell lived off of his flesh.

Packer continued with his story and said he camped with Bell under a large spruce tree near Lake San Cristobal (above what later became the town of Lake City). Both men were very hungry. Each man took opposite sides of the tree. During the still of the night, Bell tried to kill Packer with the butt of his rifle. The blow missed, and Bell, knowing he was trapped, exclaimed, "Kill me just as I intended to kill you." Packer did just that and lived off of Bell's flesh for several days before making his way to the Indian agency.

General Adams insisted that Packer guide a party of men into the mountains to verify this story. Adams promised Packer that if his story agreed with what they found, he would be released. Packer traced his trail for a while, but when he arrived at the Lake Fork of the Gunnison River leading to Lake San Cristobal, he claimed he was lost. The party found nothing and returned to the agency. Packer was placed in irons and taken to a primitive log jail in Saguache.

A second search party was sent out to find Packer's companions. They discovered two camps near Lake San Cristobal. Evidently one camp was where the entire party stopped, but the other camp was made by one man. It was obvious the second camp had been occupied for several weeks. It had a primitive shelter constructed of branches and a neat fireplace built of flat rocks. Speculation was that Packer had killed his companions and had thrown their bodies into a nearby beaver pond. By cutting through the beaver dam, the pond was partially drained, but no trace could be found of the missing men.

An artist for *Harpers Weekly* was on vacation in August, 1874, in the Lake City area and came upon a dense grove of spruce trees at the foot of a steep bluff near the banks of the Lake Fork of the Gunnison River. He was horrified to find the partially decomposed bodies of five men. Four of the bodies were lying side by side and the fifth body was nearby. The heads of the men were cut open, and blanket fibers were embedded in the wounds as though the men had been killed while sleeping. One body (later identified as that of Miller) was missing its head, and chunks of flesh had been sliced off the chest and thighs. Flesh had been hacked from at least one other body as well. The news of this discovery reached Saguache just three days after Alferd Packer escaped from the log jail.

After nine years of freedom, Alferd Packer was spotted at Fort Fetterman in Wyoming. He was living under the assumed name of John Schwartz. One of the original members of the party to journey up the Gunnison River identified him and notified authorities.

On April 13, 1883, in the Lake City courthouse, Alferd Packer was found guilty of premeditated murder and was sentenced to die by hanging on May 19. His first confession made at the Los Piños Agency was inconsistent with later confessions. According to his original story, the bodies should have been spread out among several campsites. Various witnesses testified that he had quite a bit of money with him in Saguache. A murder for money motive was emphasized by the prosecution. Packer was actually tried only for Swan's murder on the grounds that this alone would be enough to send him to the gallows. This was Hinsdale County's first death sentence and the first time in Colorado a man had been convicted of murder connected with cannibalism.

A certain humorous twist came when presiding Judge Melville B. Gerry allegedly delivered the following stern rebuke at the conclusion of the trial: "Packer, ye man-eatin' son of a bitch, they was seven dimmycrats in Hinsdale County and ye eat five of 'em, God damn ye! I sentins ye to be hanged by the neck until ye're dead, dead, dead . . . as a warnin' ag'in reducing the dimmycratic populashun in the state." Judge Gerry actually never said anything of the kind. The statement was based on an exaggerated version of comments

John A. Randolph found the remains of Alferd Packer's five companions near the present-day town of Lake City. He was a member of a sketching party roaming the West, drawing pastoral scenes. These dramatic sketches appeared in *Harper's Weekly.* (*Denver Public Library*)

by Larry Dolan, an Irish saloon keeper in Lake City. But the statement has been a source of amusement for many years.

Judge Gerry did, however, make the following descriptive statement to Alferd Packer at the close of his trial:

> In 1874 you, in company with five companions, passed through the beautiful mountain valley where stands the town of Lake City.
>
> At the time the hand of man had not marred the beauties of nature. The picture was fresh from the hands of the great Artist who created it. You and your companions camped at the base of a grand old mountain, in sight of the place you now stand, on the banks of a stream as pure and beautiful as ever traced the finger of God upon the bosom of the earth. Your every surrounding was calculated to impress your heart and nature with the omnipotence of Deity and the helplessness of your own feeble life. In this goodly favored spot you conceived your murderous designs.
>
> You and your victims had had a weary march, and when the shadows of the mountain fell upon your little party and night drew her sable curtain around you, your unsuspecting victims lay down on the ground and were soon lost in the sleep of the weary; and when thus sweetly unconscious of danger from any quarter and particularly from you, their trusted companion, you cruelly and brutally slew them all. Whether your murderous hand was guided by the misty light of the moon, or the flickering blaze of the campfire, you only can tell. No eye saw the bloody deed performed; no ear save your own caught the groans of your dying victims. You then and there robbed the living of life and then you robbed the dead of the reward of the honest toil which they had accumulated...

The Judge continued:

> For nine long years you have been a wanderer, upon the face of the earth, bowed and broken in spirit; no home, no loves, no ties to bind you to earth. You have been, indeed, a poor, pitiable waif of humanity. I hope and pray that in the spirit land to which you are so fast and surely drifting, you will find that peace and rest for your weary spirit which this world cannot give.

A stay of execution was granted to Alferd Packer on the grounds that the law under which he was found guilty was unconstitutional. During Packer's confinement in the Gunnison

Judge M.B. Gerry was supposed to have said to Alferd Packer when he was found guilty of murder and cannibalism, "Packer, ye man-eatin' son of a bitch, they was seven dimmycrats in Hinsdale County and ye eat five of 'em, God damn ye! I sentins ye to be hanged by the neck until ye're dead, dead, dead...as a warnin' ag'in reducing the dimmycratic populashun in the state." The statement actually came from a Lake City saloon keeper.

(Colorado Historical Society)

jail while the courts were debating over his final fate, many
people visited the cannibal. The jail became sort of a tourist
attraction. Packer made hair watch chains from his shoulder
length hair and curiosities from scraps of wood. He realized a
good income from the tourists. His conviction was declared
null and void due to a technicality in Colorado law between
the time of the crime and his trial. Alferd Packer was tried
again in 1886, but this time for five counts of manslaughter.
Again, he was found guilty and was sentenced to five
consecutive terms of eight years each for his crimes.

Finally in January 1901, Governor Thomas paroled him, but
reported later that Packer's letters to his relatives during his
imprisonment were "the foulest compositions I ever read
and were filled with all sorts of threats against them in the
event he regained his liberty." The parole was granted due
to Packer's poor health, but he was instructed to stay in
Colorado. Governor Thomas commented many years later, "I
don't know what became of him or when he died, but I am
very sure that he was of no use to the community and
probably a burden to himself."

Alferd Packer was found unconscious at the Cash ranch
in Deer Creek Canyon about eighteen miles southwest of
Englewood. He was suffering from epileptic fits and was
taken to the home of the widow Van Alstine. He was cared
for by the widow, and her daughter, Mrs. Cash.

The two women stayed with the sixty-four-year-old cannibal
day and night. He finally began to talk, but it was always
about his imprisonment for murders he said he did not
commit. Packer related the tragedy of his life over and over
again until the women grew indifferent to the story. For
what he had done, he felt no church could give him abso-
lution. He seemed to find no comfort in telling his story.
He seemed to state it more as a puzzle that had no solution,
and he continued to report his story over and over in a
hopeless way.

As death approached, Mrs. Cash sat by Packer's bed and
made the following observations:

His face changed strangely before he died. It began to change Wednesday afternoon. A light came into it, and it looked like a field looks when the grass waves in the wind and the sun comes out from behind the clouds. He lay in bed all the afternoon smiling, smiling like a child that dreams in his sleep. And he never smiled much before.

Alferd Packer is buried in the Littleton cemetery. The name on his tombstone reads *"Alfred* Packer"; even after his death his first name was misspelled. The plateau above Lake City is now named Cannibal Plateau.

This plaque was placed near Lake City on what was later named Cannibal Plateau to mark the spot where the remains of Packer's five companions are buried. The plaque was erected in 1928 by the Ladies Union Aid Society of Lake City.

(Kenneth Jessen)

*Closing
The Gap*

Not every eccentric story in Colorado happened during the old days. The state remains a place to find the unexpected. Bulgarian-born Christo, an artist, was in residence in 1970 at the Aspen Center of Contemporary Art. At this time, he began to survey a site for a curtain to be hung on the west side of the Continental Divide. Already to his credit was the plastic wrapping of a mile of the Australian coastline and the plastic encapsulation of several art museums. He began to survey the area for his curtain and out of eleven potential sites, picked Rifle Gap.

The town of Rifle is a small western community with a population of just over 2,000. Officials in the town were contacted in January of 1971, and they suspected that Christo was some type of escaped lunatic. What Christo proposed was a shimmering orange drapery more than a quarter of a mile long suspended from cables across the two opposing steep mountain slopes that form Rifle Gap. The curtain was to be done in the name of art, but artists are supposed to paint or create things out of clay, not hang plastic everywhere. With him, however, was Jan Van der Marck, the former director of the Chicago Museum of Contemporary Art. The townspeople began to realize that Christo was actually serious.

The money for the project came largely from European museums, as well as from Christo's sale of his drawings and models of cities. The total cost was to be $700,000. To the residents of Rifle, the curtain meant new income from tourists, the press, and the curtain workers. Also, Rifle was virtually unknown and was not exactly a hotbed of culture. Now with Christo performing one of his famous wrapping-draping works of art, Rifle knew it would become the center of attention.

The custom-made curtain was designed to fit precisely between the craggy slopes of Rifle Gap. It was a technical feat. Sewn into large vertical strips, it was fabricated from nine tons of nylon polyamide fabric. The design and installation required the technical services of a pair of engineering firms plus an industrial contractor. To give the curtain strength against the relentless winds flowing through the gap, it was hung from four steel cables 365 feet above the valley floor. The steel cables were anchored into the slopes by tons of concrete. At the curtain's base was an arched opening 37 feet high and 65 feet wide to allow traffic to flow on the state highway.

After a series of miscalculations, mishaps, and delays, August 10, 1972 arrived. It was time to put the curtain up, and the entire population of Rifle was on hand to see it. High above, suspended on a steel cable, the furled curtain hung. It was then freed from its protective cacoon. Christo was on hand, wearing a white hardhat, to direct the activity much like a conductor at a concert.

The suspense built. A little after 9:00 A.M. the wind had died to near zero. Christo gave the order to unfurl. The orange plastic began to drop by moving down along steel cables. Three-quarters of the way it snagged. "Pull! pull!" admonished Christo. Workers stationed atop the upper cable in a cage prepared to move out along the wire. Just then, a gust of wind pulled the fabric loose, and at 10:35 the curtain was down.

Like musicians after a concert, the workers were ecstatic at the results. They opened bottles of champagne and threw Christo into the cold water of Rifle Creek.

The curtain was supposed to remain in place for over a month, but twenty-four hours later a strong wind carrying sand across the arid area whipped the newly placed curtain into pieces. The untimely demise of his work of art brought no lament from Christo, however. When asked how he felt, he simply stated, "That the curtain no longer exists only makes it more interesting." When asked why he did things like this, he replied, "For me, esthetics is everything involved in the process—the workers, the politics, the negotiations, the construction difficulty, the dealing with hundreds of people. The whole process becomes an esthetic—that's what I'm interested in, discovering the process. I put myself in dialogue with other people."

(next page)

This valley curtain was the idea of Bulgarian-born artist Christo Jaracheff. Made from orange nylon polyamide fabric, it was strung across Rifle Gap. It remained in place for only twenty-four hours before the relentless wind through the gap tore it to shreds. While it lasted, it was probably Colorado's most unusual work of art.

(Leo T. Prinster)

Leadville's Short-Lived Palace

*F*or a brief period of just three months, a great palace stood on the outskirts of Leadville. Its size was stupendous. It covered an area 450 feet by 320 feet, or 3.3 acres. A pair of octagonal towers on the north side of the structure flanked the entrance. These towers had a circumference of 126 feet and stood 90 feet high. The south towers and corner towers were round and measured 60 and 45 feet high respectively. The palace had the distinctive appearance of a medieval castle. A 19-foot-high statue on a pedestal graced its entrance. The statue was of "Lady Leadville," and she pointed eastward toward the town's source of riches.

The interior of this great palace was divided into three large rooms and other smaller areas, including an exhibition hall and display rooms. In the center of the structure was a 16,000-square-foot ice skating rink. To either side of the rink were two 80-foot by 50-foot ballrooms. The east ballroom was designated the Grand Ballroom and was decorated in blue. The floors of both rooms were finished with Texas Pine. The west ballroom was decorated in orange and blue, and its primary use was as a restaurant. The inner walls of each ballroom were glassed in so spectators could watch ice skaters in the comfort of a heated area.

If its size and its location in a mountain valley at 10,000 feet above sea level weren't impressive enough, the primary construction material used to build Leadville's palace was ice! During 1895, Leadville businessmen started organizing a winter carnival to attract tourists and to put the mining camp "on the map." Originally, it was hoped to have the ice palace ready for the public by Christmas, but unseasonably warm weather almost ruined the partially complete structure. The palace was made of large blocks of ice cut from high altitude lakes in the Leadville area. A chinook wind in mid-December cut crevices in the ice walls on the shady sides, and the sun

At the entrance to Leadville's ice palace was the statue of "Lady Leadville." She pointed eastward toward the source of the town's riches. The nineteen-foot high statue was sculptured from ice and stood on a twelve-foot high pedestal.

(Denver Public Library)

softened the south walls. To save the structure, the exterior of the ice palace had to be sprayed each evening to add frozen material to the walls during the night. The repeated spraying caused the walls to take on a mother-of-pearl appearance.

After cold weather returned, the rink was flooded and made ready for skaters. The rink had wooden walls covered with ice. The ceiling was made of wood and metal trusses. The walls were lined with evenly spaced octagonal ice pillars five feet in diameter that partially hid the wooden supports. Electric lights were frozen into the pillars and walls. Moveable corner lights could be used to illuminate the frost on the ice-covered ceiling, creating the effect of thousands of sparkling diamonds.

The Leadville ice palace opened January 1, 1896. This marked the beginning of a series of parties, fireworks, outings, and general merrymaking in the mining camp. Because of its extremely high altitude, life during the winter months was typically drab, with Leadville residents looking forward to spring. Now the town had its own winter carnival. The director of the Crystal Carnival Association of Leadville wrote:

> On a massive range, where towering peaks
>   Hold white the front of the river's flow,
> We have builded (sic) a house from the Frost King's freaks,
>   And invite all the world to play in the snow.

The great, glistening castle of ice gave Leadville a chance to show the world it had "arrived." People could now realize that Leadville was more than a crude, rowdy mining camp.

Leadville readied its hotels, boarding houses, and private residences for crowds of visitors to come and enjoy their creation in ice. The railroads offered to put some of their sleeping cars on sidings to accommodate the overflow.

To kick off the opening of the carnival, January 4, 1896 was declared "Denver Day." Dignitaries and members of the press were invited to come to Leadville to see the great ice palace. The Crystal Carnival Association met the arriving newsmen at the railroad station and gave them a bucket of red paint (to paint the town red) and a key to the city.

To attract visitors, the twenty-three piece Fort Dodge Cowboy Band was hired for the first month of the carnival to play from a balcony overlooking the Grand Ballroom and skating rink. After the first month, local musicians were hired to continue the entertainment.

The ice palace also included a variety of commercial exhibits. Many of these were cleverly frozen into the walls. The breweries were well represented; after all, some of their best customers were Leadvilles's miners. Zang Brewing, Pabst Brewing, Neif Brothers Brewing, and Adolf Coors all had displays. Coors sent six barrels of bottled beer to be frozen into one of the walls of the palace as part of their display. Just in case some of the bottles broke, the brewery sent an extra case of two dozen bottles. The extra case sat around for a while, then turned up missing. A search was made for the stolen brew, and finally after two days it was discovered in another part of the palace. Out of the entire case, only half a dozen bottles had been opened, which puzzled the carnival officals. Several more bottles were opened, and it was discovered that Coors used salted water colored like beer to prevent the bottles from breaking when they were frozen into the wall. The would-be culprits must have thought that Coors had lost its ability to properly brew good beer.

Aside from the ice palace itself, there were other attractions in Leadville. Parallel to a couple of the streets were toboggan runs with heated waiting rooms. The starting point for each run was elevated to give riders an extra boost. Young boys were hired to bring the toboggans back for the next group of riders. There were tug-of-war contests, hockey tournaments, and curling contests. Local miners from other mining towns participated in rock-drilling contests. The objective was to see which team of two men could drill the deepest hole in a block of granite within fifteen minutes. At the depth of slightly over thirty-seven inches, two Leadville brothers won the contest.

The ice skating rink was the center of attention. It was kept in excellent condition by lightly flooding it with warm water

The 16,000-square-foot ice skating rink was in the center of the ice palace. To keep the ice in good condition, it was flooded daily. The ceiling was supported by trusses and the pillars along the length of the rink partially hid wooden supports within the walls. *(Denver Public Library)*

following the afternoon skating session. After three hours, it refroze ready for evening skaters. Prizes were given for the prettiest skater, the fastest skater, the most clever performance, the fanciest tricks, and so on.

Leadville's ice palace was designed to make money. Admission was 50 cents for adults, 25 cents for children, and a season ticket could be purchased for $25. The entire scheme, however, relied on partonage from Denver. The time required to get from Denver to Leadville over the two narrow gauge railroads that served the town was over nine hours one way. Many visitors arrived on a morning train with a sack lunch, paid their admission charge, enjoyed the ice palace, then returned to Denver on the evening train without spending the night. Due to Leadville's remote location, the carnival was a financial failure.

By the middle of February 1896, Leadville had grown weary of its winter carnival. The extra police hired to control the anticipated crowds were released. The merchants began to neglect snow removal, and the boardwalks became buried under tons of snow. Attendance by local people dropped off sharply.

The Crystal Carnival Association hoped it could operate the ice palace for a full three months, but on March 1, the structure began to melt because of unseasonably warm weather. Nothing could be done to halt its steady decay. On March 28 the ice palace was officially closed. The wind and sun cut the ice away from the wooden framework within its interior, and the great towers began to melt, turning the area into a sea of mud. The outbuildings were razed, and the palace's wooden framework stood throughout the summer. In mid-October, the last remnants of the ice palace were pulled down. It was an ignominious end to the largest ice structure ever built in North America.

Leadville's ice palace was located on the outskirts of town. It was constructed to attract tourists and to make money for the town. Due to lack of patronage, it was a financial failure, but it did go down in history as the largest ice structure ever built in North America. *(Colorado Historical Society)*

Time Runs Out

Colonel John Morrissey had no "learning." He couldn't read or write, or even sign his name. Never able to master figures, mathematics was a complete mystery to him. Yet his mines in the Leadville area made him rich. Armed with a bottle of his best whiskey, he went to one of his mines and shouted down the deep, dark shaft, "How many be yez down there?" The reply was, "Three." John then called down to the unseen voices below, "Well, half of yez come up and have a drink!"

Occasionally, John was called to Denver on business. Registration at a hotel posed a major problem for him, and as a result, he devised a number of methods to avoid signing his name. He would say to the room clerk, "Me fist is frose, and I kud'n howl'd a pen." The clerk would then sign for him. At one hotel, Morrissey showed up with his handkerchief wrapped around his hand. He said to the clerk, "Just write me name for me, young feller. I jist slammed the cab door on me hand and hurt it."

At the time the Twin Lakes resort was being developed near Leadville, John Morrissey was asked to express his thoughts on a weighty issue. A hotel was constructed along the water's edge. Arbors and pavilions were built in a grove of trees. As a final touch, the promoters decided to purchase some gondolas for use by their guests. When they were unable to decide on how many to buy, John was asked his opinion. "That's easy," he said. "Just get ye two and let 'em breed!"

John never wanted to admit he couldn't tell time. When he needed to know the time, he went through the following subterfuge. "Hey, Smithy, me lad," Colonel Morrissey would say, "Come on now, an tell me if I'm right in the bet I've made with meself on the time o'day." Morrissey would then hand over his large gold pocket watch and continue his dialogue. "I bet with meself it's three-thirty-five. If I'm right, we'll go into a bar an have what ever ye fancy in a drink or smoke." His friend would open the three gold covers which protected the face of the watch. As he never guessed correctly, Morrissey was always safe in his bet, and in this manner, he would find out the correct time. When Morrissey moved to Denver, most of the newspaper men came to know him and would gravely be obliged to play this pathetic game.

His watch weighed two or three pounds and was fabricated from pure gold. Its chain was formed from gold nuggets. The watch had been custom made for Colonel Morrissey in Geneva, Switzerland. It cost $1,500. Under the glass was not only a round porcelain face bearing Roman numerals and gold hands, but a miniature barometer to predict changes in the weather. The face also contained a thermometer and a calendar. A little lever on the side of the watch would actuate chimes telling the hour and the quarter hour when depressed. In the center of the stem at the top of the watch was a piston adorned with a diamond. Pressure on the diamond allowed the timepiece to be used as an accurate stop watch.

Morrissey shied away from women, but was an avid gambler. He liked horse racing. Dressed in a tailored black and white checkered sports suit and a wide-brim sombrero, he was a familiar figure at tracks all over the country. He lost much of his fortune to horse racing.

As Morrissey's mines "petered out," his money disappeared, leaving only his beautiful, Swiss-made watch. He began to look for new sources of wealth, and he was equipped as no other prospector in the long history of Colorado mining. In the back of his astonishing watch, between the outer and inner covers, was a detachable compass. The watch also had a powerful magnifying glass for use in examining ore samples.

Eventually, the watch was of no help, and to stay alive he was forced to sell the nugget chain. He mooched off his acquaintances, and finally his watch ended up in a pawn shop. John Morrissey died alone and forgotten in the Lake County poorhouse in Leadville.

Colonel John Morrissey made a fortune in the mines around Leadville
and custom ordered from Switzerland a remarkable pocket watch
made of gold. The watch was equipped like no other timepiece
in Colorado. It had chimes, a compass, a barometer, a magnifying
glass, plus many other features. Morrissey gambled away his fortune
and ended up surrendering the beautiful watch to a pawnbroker.
He died in a county poorhouse.

(Denver Public Library)

Colorado's Lightning Lab

A handsome man stood on the rolling prairie. It was night, and the stars penetrated the dark cloak of outer space. The man was dressed in formal attire. He wore a black Prince Albert coat, gloves, and a black derby. His thick-soled shoes made him seem tall.

He stood just outside an unusual barn-like structure with walls braced by wooden beams. A flimsy-looking wooden tower rose eighty feet above the ground, and from the tower a metal mast supported a three-foot copper ball over two hundred feet above the ground.

Inside the unusual building were brass bars as big as two-by-fours. In the center of the room was a gigantic cylindrical transformer wound with 40,000 feet of wire. The building was jammed with other equipment including switches, motors, cables, coils, and many other electrical gadgets.

The man in the suit was intent on watching the copper ball high above the ground. He yelled through the open door, "Czito, close the switch." Suddenly, there was a crackling sound followed by a sharp snap. Forks of blue electrical flames began to gyrate around the high sphere; then came a tremendous upsurge of power. A crescendo of loud snaps came from the tower. The noise grew quickly to resemble the staccato from a machine gun. It seemed like the building and all of its strange equipment would explode. The sound continued to build until it reached that of artillery fire and could be heard fifteen miles away. The interior of the structure was bathed in blue light from sparks dancing around the transformer. The air became ionized with strange smells, creating the illusion that perhaps the man dressed in black was the devil and had unleashed the furies of hell itself.

The flames of high voltage electrical energy began to leap from the top of the mast. At first they were only a few feet long, then, as they grew in length, they became as thick as a

KEN JESSEN

Nikola Tesla's laboratory was located just outside Colorado Springs.
It was here in 1899 that Tesla created lightning bolts 130 feet long.

man's arm. Eventually, the lightning reached down over 130 feet toward the ground.

Suddenly, the inferno of sparks stopped. The prairie was once again still. The man immediately began to scream at Czito asking him why he had opened the switch and to keep it closed. In the distance, the town of Colorado Springs was plunged into darkness.

The man in the black suit was world famous inventor Nikola Tesla, working with his assistant Kolman Czito. The building was his laboratory, where he hoped to perfect a means of transmitting messages through the air from Pikes Peak to Paris. The year was 1899.

Tesla surveyed his laboratory. It was quiet where only moments before he had stood at the apex of his career as an inventor. For a split second he had created man-made lightning using millions of volts, a feat never before accomplished and yet to be repeated.

In the meantime at the Colorado Springs Electric Company's power plant, the night operators were working feverishly to extinguish the fire in their generator. Tesla called the power company asking that his service be restored. The night supervisor flatly refused to provide Tesla with any more electricity for his crazy experiments. Only after pleading with them and offering to completely rebuild the generator did Tesla finally talk the power company into continuing his service.

Some considered Nikola Tesla to be Colorado Springs's mad scientist, but he contributed greatly to the comfort we enjoy today. He invented the most common type of motor used today, the induction motor, and the polyphase system of transmitting electrical energy. Its first practical application was at Telluride, Colorado, where a mine owner transmitted power from a hydroelectric plant to his mine high above the town. This invention became the very foundation of modern power transmission. The principles used to develop high voltage in a coil are applied today in the automobile ignition coil. Tesla also demonstrated that electrical energy could be transmitted through the air. At the distance of twenty-six miles from his laboratory, he transmitted enough energy to light 200 incandescent lamps. Tesla was also the first to recognize that radio waves originated from distant objects external to the earth.

In less than a year, Tesla was forced to abandon his work in Colorado. He ran out of money and had to return to New York to work on more practical experiments. Nevertheless, his Colorado Springs experiments with lightning of his own creation were his most spectacular accomplishments.

KEN JESSEN

Nikola Tesla was a handsome man and not afraid to take risks. His high voltage experiments were well known, but his greatest invention was the induction motor. He also invented the polyphase system of transmitting electric energy over long distances which was first tested near Telluride, Colorado.

Thompson's Tunnel

Near Loveland Pass was a place high in the mountains called Peru. During the 1800s, some men new to mining purchased the Peru claim to develop it. The first item of business was to drill a one-hundred-foot tunnel into the side of the mountain to follow a rich vein of silver ore. They hired Gassy Thompson to drill through the hard rock and to timber the tunnel. He agreed to do this for a good sum of money. The work was to be done during the winter and finished by spring. The owners left the remote high country and promised to return in the spring to inspect the work.

The first thing Gassy did was to bring in a load of timbers. Next he hired a helper and began digging. After removing the loose material from the mountainside, Gassy struck hard rock. The work was slow because drills had to be used to make holes for the dynamite. Only a few feet of rock could be removed at a time. As winter came and the snow began to fall, Gassy had a great idea. He figured out a way to dig a one-hundred-foot tunnel easily without so much backbreaking work, satisfy the mine owners, and collect all of his money. Instead of tunneling into the hard quartz, he began building the tunnel backwards using the timbers. Soon the "tunnel" stretched its full one hundred feet from the base of the mountain out into the meadow. As he and his partner erected the timbers, the snow began to drift in and covered them.

After putting all of the timbering in place, he and his partner spent a cozy winter relaxing in the mine's bunkhouse, letting nature take its course. As successive winter storms came through, the timbering became completely buried, until only the opening was visible.

When April came, the owners of the Peru snowshoed up to the mine to look over the work. They were quite pleased to see the full one hundred feet of tunnel completed. The owners inspected the tunnel, complimented Gassy on his fine timbering, and paid him in full.

It had been a severe winter, and the snow drifts didn't melt from the mountains until July. As the snow melted, the astonished mine owners saw nothing but a framework of timbers leading to a shallow hole in the side of the mountain! A search was made for Gassy Thompson, but he was far away, prospecting for more suckers.

The Prevaricator Of Pikes Peak

Sergeant John O'Keefe, an enlisted man in the U.S. Signal Corps, was sent to the top of 14,110-foot Pikes Peak in January 1876, many years before the peak became a tourist attraction. His job at this remote outpost was to operate the weather station established two years before. On the lofty summit overlooking Colorado Springs, O'Keefe spent nearly three years recording temperature, wind velocity, rainfall, and snowfall. The data he collected was transmitted via telegraph line to Colorado Springs. The Signal Corps distributed the data to local newspapers as a service. O'Keefe, however, is most noted not for the dry statistics of meteorological phenomena, but rather the astounding experiences he claimed he had on the peak.

O'Keefe warned visitors that a large number of vicious mountain rats inhabited the the rocky crevices on the summit of Pikes Peak. The rats were aggressive and dangerous. Sergeant O'Keefe said that the rats normally fed on a saccharine gum that percolated through the pores of the rocks. The gum was freed from the rock by volcanic action that shook the mountain at irregular intervals.

The most noted characteristic of the rats, said O'Keefe, was that they were seen only at night. During a full moon, he observed the rats swimming in a lake near the summit. They left a wake of sparkling light as they traversed the clear water.

One evening when the sergeant was hard at work in his office on his weather reports, he heard a scream from his wife. She ran into the room yelling, "The rats! The rats!" With great presence of mind, he immediately wrapped his wife in a sheet of zinc-plated steel. This protected her from the rats and prevented them from climbing on her. He quickly put stove pipes over his own legs. Using a heavy club, he fought the mountain rats as they entered through a window. The voracious rodents entered the kitchen and ate a quarter of beef in less than five minutes. This seemed to

heighten their appetites. They viciously attacked Mrs.
O'Keefe, and despite the protective sheet of steel, some of the
rodents managed to reach her face, leaving deep lacerations.

Right in the middle of this life-and-death struggle, Mrs.
O'Keefe grabbed a coil of wire hanging from the battery used
for the telegraph system. She made spirals on the floor by
tossing the coiled wire over to her husband. As the rats came
in contact with the wire, they were electrocuted. The rats
that survived were driven back onto the barren, rocky
summit of the mountain.

Tragically, the O'Keefe's infant child, Erin, was eaten.
Before the attack, Mrs. O'Keefe had tried her best to protect
the child by wrapping it in blankets. The mountain rats,
however, had found their way to the infant girl lying
helplessly in her crib, and all that remained was her small
skull.

The O'Keefes buried the remains of their child on the
summit of Pikes Peak and placed a marker at the head of the
grave which read, "Erected in Memory of Erin O'Keefe,
Daughter of John and Nora O'Keefe who was eaten by
mountain rats in the year 1876."

During the autumn, Sergeant O'Keefe went to Colorado
Springs for supplies. On the return to his lofty weather
station, he came across a large herd of black-tailed deer. He
estimated there were 700 animals, so many that he had
difficulty getting through the herd. O'Keefe went on to report
that it took an hour and forty minutes for them to pass a
given point!

Using his revolver, he shot seventeen animals for his meat
supply at the weather station. He tied the tails of the deer
together and slung them over the neck of his faithful
government mule, Balaam. He and his mule continued up the
steep trail until they passed timberline. They were stopped by
a large snowdrift, and O'Keefe cautiously made his way
across it. At the other side, he looked for a route up the
mountain. When O'Keefe turned and looked back, Balaam
had disappeared. The sergeant had survived the terrible raid

by mountain rats and once again faced death since all his provisions were on the back of his trusty mule.

After retracing his steps across the snowdrift, he tried to find Balaam and his supplies. The mule was in the bottom of a deep ravine and was lying with its feet in the air. It took O'Keefe some time to recover the animal, the seventeen deer, and the supplies. Darkness was approaching, and it was too late to continue on to the summit. O'Keefe and Balaam headed back to Colorado Springs.

On their way, they were ambushed by six hungry mountain lions. In order to escape, O'Keefe was forced to toss the deer to the lions. Exhausted, the sergeant and his mule reached the safety of Colorado Springs at 8:00 P.M.

In 1880, O'Keefe reported that his safety was threatened by renewed volcanic activity on the mountain. During the night, the crater near the top of Pikes Peak began to discharge vapor. When O'Keefe got close to investigate, the heat coming from the crater became oppressive and drove him back. There were signs of fresh ash and lava. The snow had melted back away from the edge of the crater.

While Sergeant O'Keefe was making weather observations from the roof of the station, a violent eruption occurred. He reported to the newpapers that it was almost as spectacular as the one he witnessed at Mount Vesuvius. He was then just a boy, and it was before he decided to leave his native country of Italy.

Lava began pouring down Pikes Peak, and soon it was near Ruxton Creek. The residents of Colorado Springs became worried that the lava might reach the creek, turning its water into steam. This was the city's only source of water.

Sergeant O'Keefe was quite proud of his thirty-two-year-old government mule, Balaam. Balaam was the first mule to climb Pikes Peak. In fact, O'Keefe claimed Balaam had made the trip 1,924 times, or an equivalent distance of 40,960 miles. Balaam also wore out 560 sets of shoes in the process.

At one time, Balaam was trapped on a rocky ridge, fighting three mountain lions. Whenever one of the lions would approach,

Balaam would strike at it with his front feet, forcing it back. If a lion tried to attack from behind, Balaam would kick it in the ribs. The trio of lions did not give up until two of them were dead, their bodies lying at Balaam's feet.

Rats don't live on the summit of Pikes Peak, and the mountain is not volcanic. There isn't a crater near the summit. It is unlikely a mule could carry seventeen deer slung across its neck. O'Keefe probably wasn't Italian. These stories were prevarications from one of Colorado's greatest storytellers, John T. O'Keefe, and they appeared in news-papers all over the United States.

Just before Christmas, 1881, Sergeant O'Keefe resigned from the U.S. Signal Corps. Before he left the Colorado Springs area, he was given a banquet and was toasted as follows:

O'Keefe, one of the greatest prevaricators, equalled by few, excelled by none. True to his record, may his life be a romance, and in his final resting place, may he lie easily.

The first toast was followed by a second,

The rosy realm of romance is as real to O'Keefe as the stern and sterile steppes of truth are to many. The golden glow which gilds the granite summit of the peak is but the type of that glamour which surrounds it through the mendacious genius of O'Keefe....Truth forever on the scaffold. Wrong forever on the throne...Gentlemen, here's looking at you.

O'Keefe, in his own day, became a Colorado folk hero. At the age of thirty-nine, John O'Keefe died suddenly. The *Rocky Mountain News* reported that, at the time of his death, he was a stoker on Steamer No. 2 for the Denver Fire Department's station on Colfax Avenue.

Sergeant John O'Keefe erected this marker at the head of the grave of what he claimed was his little girl. According to a vivid account presented by O'Keefe to local newspapers, the child was eaten by mountain rats that attacked his family at the weather station on top of Pikes Peak. It was all a hoax, and the marker was removed by a generation less given to this type of humor. *(Denver Public Library)*

Soapy Smith:
Con Man
Extraordinaire

*I*n the late nineteenth century Jefferson Randolph Smith, better known as "Soapy" Smith, and his gang of confidence men operated freely near Denver's Union Station. Beginning in 1881, Soapy had a gentleman's agreement with Denver authorities not to rob or molest its citizens. In exchange, he and his men were allowed to con the unsuspecting out-of-towners out of every cent they had.

Soapy Smith organized the "bandit barbers" of Seventeenth Street. They lured strangers into their shop by advertising a shave and haircut for only twenty-five cents. While the unsuspecting customer's eyes were covered with a steaming hot towel, the barber would flip the sign over to read $1. The customer was in no position to protest with a razor at his throat. This wasn't the end of the fleecing, however. If the victim had a fat wallet, the barber would deftly snip an inverted "V" at the hairline on the back of the neck. As he left the barber shop, another member of Soapy's gang would spot the mark and try to take him for an even more costly trimming.

Soapy Smith was one of Colorado's unforgettable characters. He had brown hair, a Vandyke beard, and a silvery voice. His most famous con was to stand in front of his small folding table at a corner along Larimer Street and attract a crowd with his repertoire of stories mixed with quick-witted comments. As he talked, he would twist a $10, $20, or even a $100 bill around a common bar of soap. He then wrapped the soap in a blue piece of paper. The crowd watched intently as he tossed the bar into a pile of identically wrapped bars on his small table. Next, he would invite the crowd to step right up and take a chance on winning "one of these little green papers with big numbers" for the ridiculous price of $5. A shill would be the first to step forward and pay the $5. Naturally, he would get one of the bars wrapped with a bill. Anxious buyers would press forward handing $5 bills to Soapy

Jefferson Randolph "Soapy" Smith was probably Colorado's greatest
con artist. He and his mob operated in Denver, Leadville, and
Creede. He got the name Soapy from an operation involving small
bars of soap. He would twist a large bill around a bar, wrap it, and
toss it into a pile with other identical bars, asking the crowd to
gamble $5 on finding it.

(Denver Public Library)

as fast as he could take the money. Few ended up with anything more than a nickel cake of common toilet soap. In a way, it was an "honest" con, and Soapy would caution the crowd to watch him carefully. His famous expression was, "Use the soap to wash away your sins! Cleanliness is next to Godliness, but the feel of a crisp greenback in the pocket is paradise."

At Seventeenth and Larimer streets, Soapy had an office on the second floor of a three-story brick building. Some of his cons required elaborate props, an office, and some great acting. He could pass himself off as a big investor in an atmosphere of dignified elegance, or some other role as required by the situation.

Soapy Smith took advantage of the greed of others, and in situations where honest people needed his help, he was more than happy to offer a hand. At Christmas, Soapy would stand at Seventeenth and Market streets and hand out turkeys to Denver's poor.

At one o'clock in the morning just a few days before Christmas, Parson Tom Uzzell heard knocking at his door. The parson opened the door and standing there was none other than Jefferson Randolph Smith. In a moment, the great con man had dumped $5,500 in gold and greenbacks on the hall floor at the parson's feet. Soapy had won it at his favorite game, faro. After reading about how the parson needed funds for Christmas, Soapy decided to give up his winnings. The money was used to feed the poor at the People's Tabernacle on Christmas day. Later, Parson Uzzell invited Soapy to deliver a sermon. It was titled "Look not Upon Evil" and was well received.

As Denver matured, its citizens became fed up with Soapy's mob rule. The handwriting was on the wall, and Soapy left for the new silver camp of Creede in 1892. The rough and tumble town was ripe for a takeover. It was easy for Soapy to make friends in a town that was gaining people at the rate of 300 per day. Many had heard of him from Denver, and he was welcomed as a celebrity. Always well dressed in his black suit and hat, Soapy became the underworld leader of Creede.

Soapy was able to maintain law and order in Creede without interfering with his own business. The headquarters for his gang was the Orleans Club. Those who came to Creede on legitimate business were welcomed by Smith, but those who tried to horn in on his rackets were dispensed with quickly. A great deal of money flowed into Soapy's pockets, and had he possessed any propensity to save, he would have ended up a rich man.

One day, a poor preacher came into the camp and began preaching from a street corner. This man of the cloth found the going rough because of the noise and disrespectful comments made by the crowd of miners. Soapy took pity on him and marched through the crowd. "Speak up, parson," Soapy said, "Creede needs a little religion. We'll back you to the limit. The town is yours." Soapy turned to some of his men and added, "Boys, we are all going to church next Sunday, and in the meantime, we are going to raise money so this man can have a church house here." Soapy's mob began visiting saloons, parlor houses, gambling halls, and other places in town. After about two hours, they delivered $600 into the hands of the dumbfounded parson. A small clapboard church was erected quickly, and Soapy Smith, with a few of his men, attended the first service.

Creede was the type of boom town that had an around-the-clock carnival atmosphere. It was the perfect setting for an inventive hoax. An imaginative fellow, Bob Fitzsimmons, found a cement body of a man in a Denver warehouse. Possibly it was the old Solid Muldoon (a hoax perpetrated in 1877 and backed by P.T. Barnum). Fitzsimmons had it shipped to Creede in a box, and during the night, hauled it a short distance from town. He buried it in the mud along Farmer's Creek. The cement man "aged" for a few days until it was "discovered" by a friend of Fitzsimmons. The discovery was reported in the local paper of April 15, 1892. Heralded as the most perfect and interesting "petrification" ever found, the cement body was hauled back to Creede and put on display at the Vaughn Hotel. Hundreds of curious people paid a quarter to view it.

Jefferson Soapy Smith was fascinated by what he quickly recognized as a good hoax. He watched for a while, but the sound of all that silver changing hands was just too much for him to resist. By manipulation, he became the owner of "Colonel Stone." This transfer of property was certainly not straightforward and was reported in the Creede *Candle* as follows:

> Jeff Smith has purchased the petrified man and will travel with him. The price was $3,000. Jeff paid the money this morning and went down to get possession. Four others claimed ownership, and it required some lively discussion with fists and guns to get away with it.

Soapy was much more of a showman than the former owner of the petrified man. He moved the cement figure into his Orleans Club and placed it in a dark area. The figure was illuminated using kerosene lamps. To create an eerie effect, the flues were partially blackened and the lamps were exposed to a slight draft to cause the flame to flicker and cast strange shadows on the figure. The dim light was also necessary because the figure was beginning to crumble.

Naturally, Soapy gave lectures about the figure to increase attendance at the attraction. The cement man had now become a prehistoric monster. Soapy talked about the creation of man and how over the centuries, he had evolved into a new kind of body. This justified the cement man's different shape.

After Soapy had milked the petrified man for every silver coin it would yield, he leased it to a circus, and the figure toured the United States. When it returned, Soapy sold it to a fellow promoter.

Eventually, the Smith regime in Creede ended, and Soapy moved to Skagway, Alaska. He tried to take over this town and was shot to death in 1898 by a member of an opposing gang. He was only thirty-eight years old and left behind just $250.

Rattlesnake
Not Served Here

*J*ohn Elitch was not only known for establishing Elitch Gardens; he also operated Denver's famous Tortoni restaurant. Every night behind the restaurant, a breadline formed. Leftover food was distributed to the poor in the alley at the kitchen door. The food from this regal establishment was an Epicurean's delight. With plenty of wildlife and the absence of game laws, hunters kept the Tortoni supplied with game and fowl. The indigent old men and women who came to the kitchen door for a handout were possibly the best-fed unfortunates in the country. They took away portions of filet mignon with sauce Bearnaise, fried oysters, filets of sole, terrapin from the Chesapeake Bay, prairie chicken, duck, quail, stuffed squab, guinea fowl breasts, sage hen, venison, elk, and bear steaks. To the older men went some of the leftover liquid refreshment. In this alley, raggedy transients would drain a bottle of Pommery or Veuve Chiquot, or a long-necked bottle of Rhenish wine, or smack their lips over the last drops of a sparkling Burgundy.

Elitch boasted that his restaurant served virtually any dish that could be purchased. One evening when the Tortoni was nearly full, two cowboys entered. They zigzagged their way across the marble tile to a table for two against a mirrored wall. With a bow, one of the highly trained French waiters presented a menu. A little tipsy, the cowboys blinked at the items listed—they were all in French. Disgusted, they threw the menu back at the waiter. One of them snarled, "Bring us a rattlesnake steak, fella, and be quick about it!"

"Pardon, M'sieu?" replied the waiter.

"Rattlesnake, I said, frog face! That's what we feed on where I come from. Good, strong, fried rattlesnake."

The waiter returned to the kitchen and repeated the order to the chef. Not knowing how to handle the situation, the chef summoned Elitch. He asked if there were any scallops on hand.

The chef's reply was, "No sir, but there is an eel in the icebox."

"Give 'em two orders of that," Elitch laughed and walked away.

After the dinner was prepared, the waiter ceremoniously brought a Sheffield silver platter to the cowboys. The platter was set in front of them. When the cover was lifted, the cheeks of the cowboys became flushed, and in their eyes was a nauseated look. Their dinner stared up at them. Simultaneously, they kicked their chairs back and, with hands held tightly over their mouths, ran for the door.

John Elitch.

Potato Clark Gets Religion

Rufus "Potato" Clark was a reformed scalawag, and he was more than happy to tell people how he "got religion." As a youth, he worked on a New England whaling ship, and after a number of adventurous years, he returned home. At the time, he referred to himself as "steeped in sin, in prodigious profanity, and the curse o'drink."

In 1859, Potato Clark came to Denver and homesteaded 160 acres in Overland Park. He became a prosperous potato farmer.

He lived a life of drinking, carousing, and, as he put it, "dancing the sailor's hornpipe on the streets and singing chanteys in a voice that boomed like thunder." Clark was shunned by the respectable and followed by the disreputable.

In the summer of 1873, a noted evangelist, Rev. E.P. Hammond, held an oldtime revival in Denver. Potato Clark, "under the influence," stumbled into the meeting by accident and demanded to be taken to the front bench. Room was made for him. He sat directly under the evangelist's fiery eyes. The preacher thundered from the front of the room, holding up Potato Clark as an example of what "the demon rum can do to a man created in the image of his Maker."

Befuddled, Potato shouted, "Hear! Hear!"

His shouting was met with hisses from the congregation. Their reaction was something new to him, because in the past, crowds had always been amused by his antics. Clark began to pay attention to what Rev. Hammond was saying about him. As his head cleared, he endorsed the evangelist's excoriation. And when the time came, he was the first to rise and openly confess his sins to the congregation. His confession was met with "Amen, brother," and "Praise the Lord." From that moment on, Potato Clark dedicated himself to religion.

Clark became a one-man Salvation Army walking Denver's streets, singing "Rock of Ages." He preached from the street corners and announced his reformation. His friends didn't believe him. Roars of laughter interrupted his renunciation of sin. He managed to hold his temper, but kept his fists tightly clenched in his pockets. He tounge-lashed his erstwhile drinking buddies until they were left wondering what had happened to Potato.

Naturally, his friends predicted he would backslide, but Potato kept his pledge by avoiding drink and devoting himself to farming. He became the largest property owner in Arapahoe County and paid taxes on 4,500 separate holdings. The listing of his property required a dozen pages in the assessor's book. In 1886, he used his wealth to build the Rufus Clark and Wife Theological Training School on Africa's west coast. For the rest of his life, he was a trustee of the University of Denver, a school he founded with $500 and a donation of eighty acres.

Rufus "Potato" Clark is credited with founding the University of Denver with a $500 donation plus eighty acres of land. Prior to this, he "got religion" at an oldtime revival.

(Colorado Historical Society)

*Highest Fort
in the
United States*

*E*xtreme situations call for extreme solutions. Fort Peabody was constructed at 13,400 feet in the San Juan Mountains of Southern Colorado to guard Imogene Pass. In 1893, the Western Federation of Miners was organized and began a campaign for better wages, shorter hours, and safer working conditions. In 1901, miners in the Telluride mining district won the right to work an eight-hour day. Disputes continued, however, between the union and the mineowners over higher wages. This led to violence, including several murders.

At the reduction mills and cyanide plants in Telluride, about 100 men went on strike September 1, 1903. They wanted their workday reduced from twelve to eight hours, to equal that given to the miners. The millworkers also wanted a new wage scale of between $3 and $4 a day. With the mills shut down, there was no place to process the ore, and Telluride's mining industry came to a halt. Soon the union miners joined the millworkers and went on strike.

The mineowners asked Colorado Governor James H. Peabody to send troops to maintain law and order. The hope of the minowners was to reopen using nonunion workers. Governor Peabody responded by asking President Theodore Roosevelt for 300 army regulars. The request was turned down. On November 20, 1903, Governor Peabody dispatched 500 National Guardsmen to Telluride. The men were "flatlanders" from Lamar and Rocky Ford, towns on Colorado's eastern plains. The troops arrived November 24 via the Rio Grande Southern Railroad, and set up camp.

It wasn't long before forty strikers were arrested for vagrancy and "deported" to Ridgway. The rail fare for the forty-five mile trip was paid by the county.

Army Major General J.C. Bates made an inspection tour of Telluride to report back to President Roosevelt. He concluded that "the disturbances amount to insurrection against the state of Colorado." As more miners were deported, the union president called President Roosevelt, asking for protection for his men. There was no response. Union unrest came to a boil when the mineowners reopened using scab labor. On January 3, 1904, twenty-two union men were arrested and deported. As the weeks passed, more and more union men were sent out of Telluride.

Telluride officials began to note that some of the deportees were second-time and even third-time offenders. Guardsmen carefully watched all incoming traffic, including trains and wagons. The only way these union men could be infiltrating was over 13,114-foot Imogene Pass. Mine-owners and guardsmen headed up the pass with timbers to erect an enclosed gunner's nest to stop the union miners. The primitive fort was surrounded by a breastwork of rock and was located overlooking the pass.

Troops were posted in this lofty fortification and were under orders to stop and investigate all traffic over the pass. It is a wonder they survived. The fort was located well above timberline and was exposed to high winds. Temperatures, even during the day, might have been well below zero. Although not an official military installation, the fort was named in honor of Governor Peabody. After Telluride was secured, the troops were withdrawn and military control was turned over to a mine manager. He was an ex-army captain and had organized the Telluride vigilante committee. His men went on a rampage and forced their way into many homes to rout union sympathizers. Many men were rounded up and deported. A week later, Governor Peabody was forced to impose martial law, and sent the National Guardsmen back to Telluride. He declared San Miguel County in a state of insurrection.

Using Fort Peabody to keep any infiltrators from coming in the back door, Telluride had only to worry about its front door. On April 8, 1904, seventy-four miners boarded a train at Ridgway for the trip to Telluride. They planned to force their way into town and drive the nonunion workers out.

Although not an official military installation, Fort Peabody was manned by National Guardsmen during 1904 to prevent union sympathizers from entering Telluride through the "back door" over Imogene Pass. The fort was located at an elevation of about 13,400 feet, and temperatures, even during the day, might have been well below zero. *(Denver Public Library)*

The train arrived early in the morning, but the guardsmen had been tipped off, and a heavily armed welcome party, consisting of 100 soldiers and 200 citizens, met the train. The union miners were disarmed, fed lunch, and "redeported" on the next train.

Finally, after fourteen months, the mineowners conceded, granting the miners an eight-hour shift and a new wage scale of $3 to $4 per day. Fort Peabody was abandoned, ending an unusual chapter in the unofficial military history of the United States.

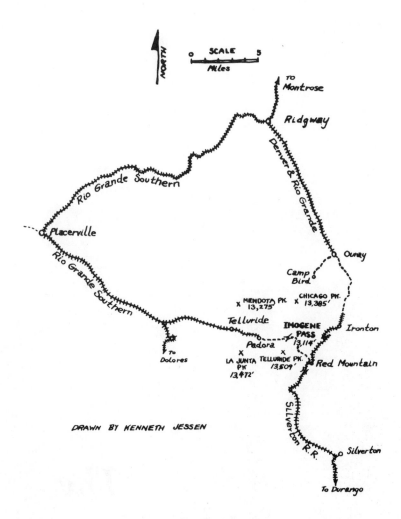

DRAWN BY KENNETH JESSEN

The Solid Muldoon

Southern Colorado has always been a rich area
for archaeologists, naturalists, and geologists.
Ancient pottery, tools, and even the remains of humans have
been found there.

On September 20, 1877 Mr. William A. Conant traveled
through the country southwest of Pueblo, and in the process
discovered a variety of fossils, including a sea turtle in an
excellent state of preservation. He continued his search for
more fossils and arrived in Pueblo with a large stone figure of
a man. His startling discovery made the headlines in practically every Rocky Mountain newspaper. The stone figure
was found near the head of a long, dry arroyo about twenty-
five miles from Pueblo. Conant related that he had to use a
pick to free the figure from the hard clay. A cedar tree had
extended its root between the arm and body of the figure,
proving, said Conant, that it had been there for centuries.

Mr. Conant explained to the press that his discovery was
made while he ate lunch. He spied a curious-looking stone
protruding from the ground. Removing some of the loose clay,
he found what resembled a human foot. At this point, he
began to remove the clay to expose the entire figure.
Unfortunately, in removing the figure from its grave, the head
broke off at the neck.

Speculation was that the figure was the petrified body of a
man, but others thought it was a piece of ancient sculpture
because the figure seemed to be composed of a slatelike rock.
It had a dirty yellow color which was believed to be from its
centuries of contact with the surrounding clay.

The statue was of a man in a reclining position with one
arm crossed over the breast and the other lying along its side
with the hand resting on the leg. The height of the giant was
seven-and-a-half feet, and it weighed around 450 pounds.

Mr. Conant speculated on what type of human race the
body represented. The face had Asiatic features with high

cheekbones. The figure was thin, much like men in ancient Egyptian pictures. The most remarkable feature of all was a tail about two inches long at the end of the backbone. The arms were apelike in appearance and, if straightened, would reach below the knee. The feet were long and flat. The big toe was a full two inches shorter than the middle toes. Newpapermen added that this creature was strongly suggestive of the truth of the Darwinian theory and could very well be the long-sought-after "missing link" between man and ape.

Upon examination by experts, there appeared to be no doubt that the figure was genuine. The stone showed all the effects of time, and the circumstances of the discovery seemed to fit into place.

The Colorado Giant was dubbed the "Solid Muldoon" and became the chief topic of the day. It was said to be one of the new wonders of the world, and people from all over the United States came to examine it in a Pueblo theater.

E. Shelburne, editor of the Pueblo *Colorado Weekly Chieftain*, was skeptical, especially after a visit by Phineas Taylor Barnum to see the Solid Muldoon. Barnum had established himself by exploiting his fellow man. To say the least, he was an accurate judge of American susceptibility to suggestion. Shelburne set out with three other men to visit the would-be discovery site. The location was halfway up a small hill. The earth was composed of shale right down to the bottom of the excavation. A sign had been left behind by Conant which read, "This mount is given the name of Ancient Mount, named by W.A. Conant. A petrified man or beast was found here by me."

The men, under the direction of the editor, looked at the bottom of the excavation for some indentation produced by the long repose of the solid stony form. They were unable to discover any hint that the Solid Muldoon had ever been there. As for the root that supposedly had grown between the arm and the body, the largest root that entered the excavation measured no more than three-eighths of an inch across.

Shelburne smelled a rat and concluded, "It would be almost

as much impossible for that stony form to lay imbedded in the earth and leave no impression as it would be for a tree to make no shade when the sun was shining on it. In fact, the whole thing is too thin, and smells of P.T. Barnum."

A reporter from the Kansas City *Times* interviewed P.T. Barnum regarding Mr. Conant's find. It is interesting to note how little information was obtained in the interview. The reporter began by asking, "Mr. Barnum, is the Pueblo Petrification a real, solid, bona fide stone man, or is it another Cardiff Giant (a hoax perpetrated in 1869)?"

"I believe it to be just what it is represented to be," Barnum began. "If I had not, I would not have offered Mr. Conant $20,000 for it."

"Did you really offer the owner that amount of money for it?"

"I did, and he refused it," Barnum said emphatically. "But he offered to sell me three-fourths and retain one-fourth interest in it."

"So you feel assured, Mr. Barnum, that this new discovery is what it is claimed to be—a real petrified man?"

"No. I won't say that it is a petrified man, but either man or beast petrified into stone. I feel sure of this, because in the excavation or resurrection of the stone corpse, the head broke from the shoulders and there was a weathered, crystalized spine and other bones as natural as life. Oh, no, sir, I am sure that this is no Cardiff Giant affair."

"How does it look?" continued the reporter.

"Well, sir, it is a well-defined human body petrified into solid stone. The most singular part of it is its tail, which is well defined and an unmistakable part of the body. . ."

"Perhaps it is a petrified gorilla, Mr. Barnum?" interrupted the news gatherer.

"No, no, I do not think so. The cheek bones are high and projecting, like the American Indian, and the formation of hands and feet indicate that it is not of the monkey species."

The reporter grew more excited as Barnum added the icing to the cake. "What do you think it is?"

"Well, sir, it is my candid opinion that in this discovery we have found the missing link which Darwin claims connects mankind with the beast creation. It is certainly the petrified body of a man with a tail, and was dug up by an old man named W.A. Conant near Pueblo."

"Is he a reliable party, Mr. Barnum? Perhaps it is a put-up job on you and the public."

"Yes, he is reliable. He is a respectable old man and is an agent for the Atchison, Topeka & Santa Fe Railroad. He was once a member of the New York legislature, and is much respected in Colorado where he had lived for several years. He says he will not sell the petrification until it has been examined by Professor Marsh (a prominent anthropologist of the day) or some other authority."

P.T. Barnum continued his journey back to his palatial home in Bridgeport, Connecticut.

On October 25, 1877 the Pueblo *Colorado Weekly Chieftain* decided to publish the opinion of Professor John L. Boggs, a noted phrenologist, who lived about seven or eight miles from the site of the find. Professor Boggs, a resident of the territory for seventeen years, was considered to have sound judgement. The colorful report by Professor Boggs reads, in part, as follows:

> Will you please give me space. . .to give the public a few graphic ideas in reference to that gigantic and formidable man, spectre, apparition, ghost, or image, that was exhumed in Colorado on September 20, 1877, by Mr. Conant of Colorado Springs, measuring seven feet eight inches in height; said form being nearly perfect except for a rent diagonally across the sternum, exposing some of the respiring (sic) organs? Yes, some people a little more imaginary, say they saw him breathe as he lay on his couch in Pueblo, in the old theatre building. So perfect were his smiles of congratulation that the over spiritual on entering the room would almost say, "Howdy, Mr. Petrified Indian."
>
> . . .I have visited the tomb in person, and Dr. Shelburne, Mr. Struile, Mr. Laking, and others from Pueblo have also paid a visit lately to the mound of ancient idols and of the heathen aborigine. . . . And in all examinations yet made

around the giant's grave not a piece of ancient armor had ever been found, such as a sceptre, crown, shield, lance, spear, bow, quiver, gun, butcher knife, nor tomahawk. Such armor, all or in part, would surely have been used by this giant king of the Lamonites. . .or more modern aborigines, who seldom ever bury their dead without them.

But this body was not well proportioned, for the three lower vertebrae protrude, and the. . .hand reached clear below the capula joints, and the matter is in great doubt whether this is not similar to some objects of sculptured work in stone to be found in modern times by the antiquarian along the Nile in the form of the Sphinx. . . . You will please allow me to differ from scientists if they should pronounce him a real petrified Indian of the Rocky Mountains.

But it is no different whether an idol, image, or rock, is surely a magnificent humbug for Barnum.

Your title, race, or blood,
Say, did you live before or since the flood?
It was a mighty blunder,
When this statue fell asunder.
  (signed)
  Prof. Boggs

Mr. Fitch was the proprietor of a factory for manufacturing artificial stone using what was known as the "Rollins carburated stone process." His plant was located in the northern part of Connecticut.

Mr. Hull, the very same individual who sculptured the magnificent ten-foot Cardiff Giant in 1869, contacted Mr. Fitch in February 1876. After the two men talked for a while, Hull offered Fitch money to aid in the creation of what he referred to as a "new curiosity." Hull's Cardiff Giant had been exposed as a hoax in 1870, and now he was ready to tackle a new project. He told Fitch he wanted to get some bones cast into the figure for authenticity, but did not know how. Fitch said he could manage it.

A secret plant was set up in an icehouse leased by Hull on a farm in Pennsylvania. Hull began by making molds for the petrified man while Fitch did the casting. The molds of the lower portion of the body were taken from Hull's son-in-law.

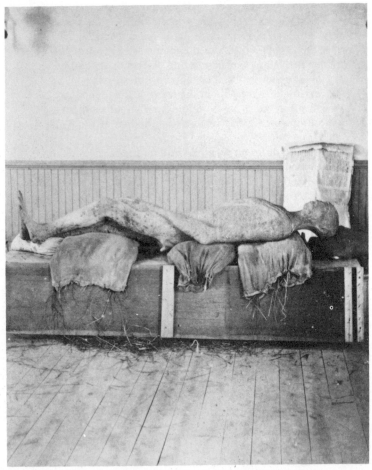

One of the West's greatest hoaxes was the Solid Muldoon. It was "discovered" near Pueblo and was passed off as a petrified man. It measured over seven feet and was actually cast out of Portland cement. At the base of the spine the figure had a short tail, and the Solid Muldoon was touted as Darwin's "missing link."

(Denver Public Library)

He was a slender young fellow over six feet tall with long legs and arms. Sections of approximately a foot in length were molded by Hull, and immediately filled with Portland cement by Fitch. The marks where the sections joined were clearly visible, even later when the Solid Muldoon was on exhibition. Fitch could not conceive of how these people apparently failed to notice them.

Everytime another segment was cast, Hull's son-in-law had to strip. The ice house was very chilly, and the model constantly complained, then finally walked off the job. Hull had to use his own body to make the casts of the upper portion of the figure. Hull's build, however, was the exact opposites of his son-in-law's. Hull was short, thickset, and had a large chest. This, of course, accounted for the disproportion of the figure.

The statue was built in an erect position using Portland cement mixed with brown pigment. After a molded section was completed, it would be placed into position and stuffed with cement.

A human skeleton was purchased, and portions of it were utilized in various parts of the statue where examinations would likely be made by scientists. Bones were placed all the way up both legs. and a straight bone was stuck in the lower portion of the back with an inch protruding to keep the tail from breaking off. To strengthen the upper part of the body, the shin bone from a cow was inserted through the neck from the middle of the head down to the center of the chest. A piece of skull was placed in back of the left ear, where later the statue was bored to prove its authenticity. In case scientists looked for a backbone, some ground bones were moistened, rolled into little lumps, and placed down the middle of the back.

The completed figure was laid on a brick platform above a furnace. Over the platform was a tentlike structure. Fitch burned charcoal to make carbonic acid gas. The gas was trapped by the tentlike structure and surrounded the figure. The gas acted on the moist cement and turned it into a stonelike material after about a week. At the time, this process was little known by scientists. The cement used to create the Solid Muldoon cost only $11.45.

Despite this economy, Hull used all of his money—about $6,000—during the construction of the statue. He contacted P.T. Barnum to see if he would be interested in investing in the hoax. Barnum sent an agent to examine the statue. The agent's report was satisfactory, and Barnum purchased part interest in it. After all, it was his motto that "a sucker is born every minute."

The statue was shipped to Colorado Springs in a machinery crate. W.A. Conant, an employee of Barnum, received the shipment and arranged to have it transported out into the countryside near Pueblo to be "discovered." Barnum made sure he was in Colorado shortly after the discovery to play the role of an interested investor.

Two noted professors were hired by Barnum to examine the statue and make a report. They had no idea they were part of a scam. Hull traveled from Connecticut to assist the professors and listened carefully to what tests they would make. He learned that if the Solid Muldoon were truly a petrified man, calcite crystals would likely be found in its interior. Hull volunteered to do the boring and, without being observed, carefully held some calcite crystals between his thumb and forefinger. He slowly introduced the crystals into the material which came from the statue and hoodwinked the learned men.

After its stay in Pueblo, Barnum arranged to have the Solid Muldoon transported to the New York Museum of Anatomy. This museum was owned by Barnum, and more scientists were allowed to examine it. This time, they demanded that a second bore be made into the stomach area. Hull was kept busy at night chiseling a hole into the stomach, then inserting a number of calcite crystals. The hole was then covered with some colored Portland cement and hardened. But Fitch couldn't stand the burden of secrecy, and just before the scientists were going to cross-section the stomach area, he exposed the hoax.

The Hermit of Pat's Hole

At the point where the Yampa River meets the Green River is a mile-long fin of rock, and the canyon walls are nearly vertical here. The Green River flows in opposite directions around this fin. John Wesley Powell named the area Echo Park, because the opposing canyon walls created an extraordinary echo. As put by Powell, "Standing opposite the rock, our words are repeated with startling clearness, but in a soft, mellow tone that transforms them into magic music. Scarcely can you believe it is the echo of your own voice." This area also had another visitor, and another name.

Pat Lynch was born in Ireland and, as a teenage boy, worked on a sailing ship. He was shipwrecked on the coast of Africa and captured by a native tribe. After several years, he was rescued. He traveled to the United States, enlisted in the U.S. Navy under the name of James Cooper, and fought in the Civil War. He was badly wounded when trying to toss a live shell overboard after it landed on the deck of his ship. Later, he enlisted under his own name in the Union Army. After the Civil War ended, Pat Lynch drifted to Denver, then to Brown's Park. Lynch was hired to hunt game for Major Powell's survey party.

In 1883, Pat moved to the isolated northwestern corner of Colorado. Some say it was to escape prosecution for murder. For a short time, he lived in a cabin near the mouth of Hell's Canyon. While he was out getting some water, the cabin blew up. A possible cause could have been old dynamite stored in the cabin. Very suspicious by nature, Pat thought someone was after him, so he moved into a shelter cave along the Yampa River. He then started moving from cave to cave. During his occupation of each cave, he drew crude pictures of boats on the walls.

Eventually, Lynch settled at the confluence of the Yampa and Green rivers between Lodore Canyon and Whirlpool

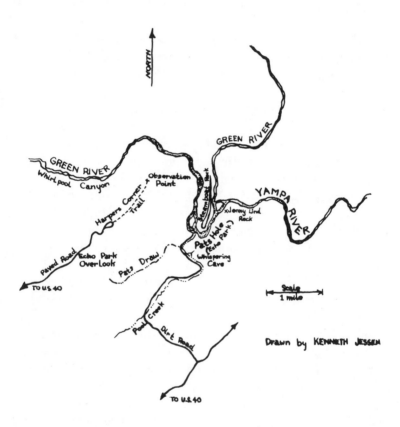

Canyon. The area named Echo Park by Powell became known as Pat's Hole. Here he constructed a lean-to covered with willow branches. This was all the shelter he had for many years until some local cowboys built a proper cabin for him.

Lynch didn't believe in killing animals, even though he had hunted at one time. He made pets of many of the wild creatures in the area, and he lived like a coyote by eating the flesh of dead animals he found in the river. He made jerky out of most of the meat. To allow him to travel light, he had jerky and bread cached throughout the area. When riding with a friend, he was known to stop and study the canyon for a minute. He would then walk over to a crack in the wall, or a rock, and recover some meat and bread. Naturally, some of it was pretty old.

Tales of Pat's close friendship with a mountain lion were widespread. He claimed he tamed this lion, and the big cat would frequently leave a dead deer by his cabin. He could call the lion with a peculiar wail. The lion would answer with a scream from the cliffs above Pat's Hole. Pat described the lion's scream by saying, "That sound is sweeter than any Jenny Lind ever sang." One of the cliffs in the area is now known as Jenny Lind Rock.

Pat Lynch continued to maintain his little twenty-five acre ranch and planted a few peach trees. He also had a small garden and a couple of shacks. The bearded old man rode many miles to the nearest post office to collect his pension for service in the Civil War. He was fond of recounting his experiences to any visitor who would listen. Nearly deaf, he paid little attention to comments made by others during the middle of a good story. He kept up on the news by reading *New York World*, *Collier's Weekly*, and the *Literary Digest*.

As he grew older, he scarcely knew what he was talking about. He rambled from one subject to the next. Visitors would listen with impatience to hear the end of some wonderful tale. Then he would suddenly switch to an entirely different subject, leaving the first story unfinished.

Pat was constantly drawing sailing vessels. Some of his

drawings are carved into the canyon walls. His body was elaborately tattoed. When he was in the right mood, he told people he killed a man in Pittsburgh and fled to the West to escape punishment. It may have been a joke or a means of shocking visitors.

During the last three years of his life, the hermit of Pat's Hole lived with friends. He died in 1917 at the age of ninety-eight.

After Pat's death, a small scrap of paper was found in one of the caves he occupied on Upper Pool Creek. Written on the paper was the following message:

> To all who this may consarn (sic) that
> I Pat Lynch do lay claim on this bottom
> for my home and support this 8th
> > month of 1886
> >   (signed) P. Lynch
> If in these caverns you shelter take
> Plais (sic) do to them no harm
> Love everything you find around
> Hanging up or on the ground.

Pat Lynch lived at the confluence of the Yampa and Green rivers. The area was named Echo Park by John Wesley Powell, but it was also known as Pat's Hole. Pat's hard life and seclusion must have agreed with him, since he reached the age of ninety-eight.

(Colorado Historical Society)

I'll Dance on Your Grave

As Sheriff George O'Connor lay on his death bed, Martin Duggan was appointed the new marshall of Leadville to replace him. O'Connor was shot in the line of duty, and Duggan was hired to rid Leadville of its criminal element. With his Irish background and a boyhood spent on the streets of New York City, Duggan was the right man for the job. He arrived in Leadville in 1878 and became marshall that same year.

If ever a law officer of a frontier town had his work cut out for him, it was Martin Duggan. The criminal element had eliminated his two predecessors at the rate of one a month, and soon after Duggan became marshall, he received written notice that he was to leave town or suffer the same fate. Duggan was a product of the era he lived in, and he used the same methods to tame Leadville that the criminals used to terrorize it. It was a case of fighting fire with fire. With little regard for the letter of the law, his determination and muscles allowed him to establish order in Leadville. When confronting an outlaw, Duggan made it clear that he had a choice of instant death or imprisonment.

Martin Duggan was so effective that over a thousand Leadville residents ended up in "crowbar hotel" during his first few months as sheriff. Crimes included murder, rape, bigamy, adultery, robbery, riot, forgery, assault, and vagrancy.

In the spring of 1880, Duggan resigned as marshall and went into the livery business. On Monday, November 22, he was asked to deliver a sleigh to Winnie Purdy. She was one of Leadville's ladies of pleasure and lived in the red light district. Duggan set out across the fresh snow in a sharp-looking sleigh pulled by a pair of equally good-looking black horses. As he neared the corner of Pine and Fifth, he almost knocked down Louis Lamb. The two men exchanged a few heated words, and Duggan drove off. This should have ended the matter, but his hot Irish temper got the best of him, and Duggan turned the sleigh. Once he reached Lamb he demanded and apology. Lamb elected to let his revolver do his talking. This was a mistake, because Duggan dropped to the ground behind one of his horses and shot Lamb through the mouth. Lamb died instantly and fell to the ground with his pistol still cocked. Martin voluntarily surrendered to the police captain and later was found innocent by virture of self-defense. Ironically, Duggan had never killed a man during his term as marshall.

Louis Lamb was a local miner and a family man. His wife vowed eternal hatred for the ex-marshall, and she promised to wear her "widow's weeds" until he was dead. She then vowed to dance on his grave and deliver her "widow's weeds" to Duggan's wife.

After he killed Lamb, Duggan's business went downhill and finally failed in 1882. He left Leadville only to return in 1887 to work as a policeman. In April of the following year, Duggan was in the Texas House. At this popular gambling establishment, he got into an argument with owner Bailey Youngson. Duggan was drunk and upset with one of the dealers for some unknown reason. He threatened to run the fellow out of town. When Youngson attempted to defend his dealer, Duggan asked him to get his gun and meet him out in the street.

Duggan's friends persuaded him to leave and go home. At around three-thirty in the morning a shot rang out, and several men began shouting for the police. They found Martin Duggan lying in a pool of his own blood on the boardwalk in front of the Texas House. A bullet had entered his head behind the right ear, and it was amazing that he was still alive. The powder burns indicated that he was shot at close range.

At daylight, Duggan regained consciousness. He was asked who shot him. He said it was Bailey Youngson, but later said he didn't know. He did indicate that it was "one of the gang." The ex-marshall passed away at 11:00 A.M., April 9, 1883. It was almost ten years to the day from the time he began serving as marshall of Leadville.

Louis Lamb's widow did deliver her "widow's weeds" to Mrs. Duggan as promised. She did not dance on Martin Duggan's grave, but danced in front of the Texas House where he had been shot.

La Caverna Del Oro

*H*igh in the Sangre de Cristo ("Blood of Christ") Mountains above the Wet Mountain Valley is La Caverna del Oro ("The Cavern of Gold" also known as Spanish Cave). The cave entrance is above timberline on the side of a ravine in an area known as Marble Mountain. The entrance is usually blocked by a large snow drift that does not melt until August. Snow often comes to the Sangre de Cristos in September, leaving the cave accessible for only a month or less. A strong wind blows through its subterranean passageways, and its floors are covered with ice or mud. The walls weep with water. This is not a pleasant cave to explore, since it consists of a series of steep tunnels and vertical shafts or pits. Much equipment and endurance is required to penetrate La Caverna del Oro.

Stories of this cave began before the Spaniards arrived on the North American continent. As passed from generation to generation, legends tell of gold in the cave. The Indians discovered the gold and used it as an offering to their gods. Eventually, the gods became angry, and mining in the cave was abandoned. Spanish monks recorded this legend.

La Caverna del Oro was not mentioned again until 1541. Seeking a mythical city, three monks journeyed north from Mexico. After the death of two monks, the remaining friar found the cave with the help of the Indians. He promised to share with them its riches. Once the monk and his fellow Spaniards arrived, the Indians were tortured and forced into slavery. Much gold was brought to the surface from the depths of the cavern. After loading the gold on the pack animals, the Spaniards were said to have massacred the Indians.

Another version of this story tells that the Indians revolted against the Spaniards. The Spaniards were forced to construct a fort in front of the lower cave entrance for protection. By using ladders within the cave's passageways, the Spaniards climbed to the upper entrance and surprised the Indians from

The entrance to La Caverna del Oro is above timberline at an elevation of about 12,000 feet. During most of the year, it is blocked by snow drifts.

(Lloyd E. Parris)

behind. The Indians were killed, and the gold was taken back to Mexico.

La Caverna del Oro remained hidden until 1811, when a Spanish-American named Baca stumbled across a pile of nuggets and gold bars high in the Sangre de Cristo Mountains. He searched for the source of the metallic riches, but could find no trace of a mine.

In 1869, Elisha Horn explored Marble Mountain and rediscovered the cave. Supposedly, he found a skeleton clad in Spanish armor. An arrow had pierced the armor, killing its occupant. The skeleton was discovered near the cave's entrance.

The cave remained in obscurity until 1880. J.H. Yoeman located the cave once again and described an ancient fortress at the mouth of a smaller cave a few hundred yards below the entrance to La Caverna del Oro. The walls of the fort were constructed of rock and timbers. Rifle pits surrounded the breastwork. The Spanish legend seemed to have some truth to it.

The cave came back into focus in 1920, when a couple of forest rangers learned of it from Mrs. Apollina Apodaca, a descendant of the first Spanish explorers in the area. Mrs. Apodoca recited the legend of La Caverna del Oro. Her version included the revolt by the Indians after being enslaved by the Spaniards. She also told how people would visit the cave and throw blankets into the entrance. The perpetual wind coming out of the cave would carry the blankets back to their owners. She also added that at a depth of ninety feet, the Spaniards dug a tunnel back into the mountain to reach the gold.

The forest rangers located and entered the legendary cave. They were unable to go beyond the top of the first pit because they lacked enough rope. They did find a dull red Maltese cross painted on a rock near the cave's entrance. They also confirmed that a cold wind came from the cave.

The legend of La Caverna del Oro moved further away from fantasy and more toward reality in 1929. An expedition was

A dull red Maltese cross painted on a rock marks the entrace to La Caverna del Oro ("The Cavern of Gold"). The cross may have been put there in the 1500s by the Spaniards to mark the cave's entrance. *(Lloyd E. Parris)*

financed by Frederick G. Bonfils, co-founder and publisher of the Denver *Post*. He wanted to see if the legends were based in fact. The expedition consisted of two men, and after they explored the cave, a report was published.

The men reported that the cave's steep passageways were either covered with water, ice, or mud. The intense cold and ceaseless wind nearly froze their wet gloves. At the brink of a deep pit, an ancient log was wedged between the walls. An iron chain ladder was fastened to the log. The chain was very old and nearly rusted through. The walls of the cavern were composed of deep red marble with streaks of gray. The men lacked sufficient rope to fully explore the cave; in fact, they covered only a small percentage of it. No evidence was found of gold or of mining activity.

In 1932, another attempt was made to explore the cave. This time, the party took quite a bit of rope. Deep inside Marble Mountain, after descending quite a distance, a lantern was lowered on a rope into a deep pit. At the bottom was a skeleton with a metal strap around its neck. It appeared that some poor individual had been chained by the neck to the wall of the cave and left to die.

News of the exploration was published in the *Rocky Mountain News* and generated so much interest that a second group visited La Caverna del Oro the following weekend. This group of seven men included some of Colorado's best-trained cavers. They solved some of the mysteries, but added new ones. During the week between visits to the cave, someone attempted to dynamite the entrance shut. It is possible that this was done to keep people out, for fear the legendary gold would be found. Numerous Indian arrowheads were found at the fort built below the cave's entrance. This supported the theory that the Indians revolted and attacked the Spaniards.

The party of seven descended the first drop estimated to be a full 250 feet (later surveyed at 175 feet). At the bottom of this pit, primitive ladders made of tree trunks inset with pegs were found. No nails were used in their construction.

After traveling deeper into the mountain through steep, icy

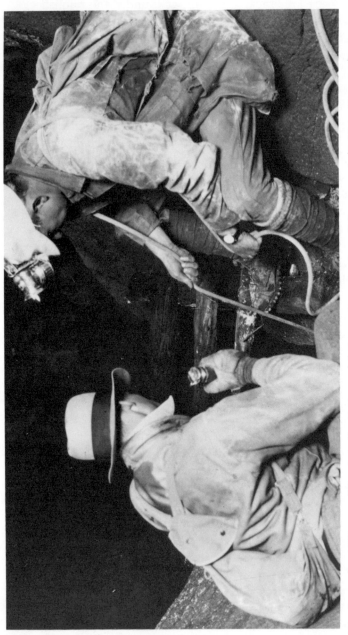

Members of a 1932 expedition into La Caverna del Oro wait at the top of the second pit. Note the wooden framework said to have been used by the Spaniards to hoist gold ore. *(Denver Public Library)*

passageways, the party came to another pit. Over the top of this shaft, a wooden structure was built that could have been used to hoist ore. Members of the party could not see the bottom of this pit, even after tossing a flare into the hole. Using a rope, its depth was established at 110 feet. Dr. LeRoy Hafen, curator of the Colorado State Historical Society, and one other man were lowered into the shaft. Because of an overhanging lip, the rest of the party had to stay on top to hoist the men out. At the bottom, Dr. Hafen and his companion failed to find the skeleton, but they did bring up a hand-forged hammer. It was later identified by Dr. Hafen as seventeenth-century vintage. Reaching out from this level were more passageways. Each ended in yet another deep pit.

Local guides accompanied this party and confirmed rumors of the skeleton and the iron chains attached to tree trunks to form ladders. One legend proclaimed that at the very bottom of the cave are two large wooden doors that guard the hidden treasure.

An article published in 1935 in *American Forest* magazine reviewed many of the facts about La Caverna del Oro. The article, however, added a new legend. A skeleton, hung on a wooden cross, once guarded Marble Cave near La Caverana del Oro. As the story goes, a trapper wandered near the cave, and to protect their interests, the Spaniards crucified him. For half a century, his bones remained on the cross. Members of the Fremont expedition gave the poor fellow a decent burial. Legend stipulates that the trapper's ghost haunts the cave.

A piece of human bone was recovered in 1959 from a pool in the cave. Another expedition found a bundle of dynamite dangling over the first pit. Someone chiseled away part of the Maltese cross, and strange lights have been seen in the vicinity of the cave.

Lloyd E. Parris in his excellent book, *Caves of Colorado* (Pruett, Boulder, Colorado, 1973), concludes that even now the cave resists all intruders. Everything seems to go wrong when attempts are made to explore La Caverna del Oro. Cavers become sick, or basic caving techniques are momentarily forgotten. Most attempts to solve the riddles only tend to complicate them. Only during the last few years has the cave been fully explored. Many of the legends now seem believable, but what about the lost gold? Why haven't any of the expeditions found evidence of mining? Are there two doors at the very bottom to guard the treasure? The final chapter of La Caverna del Oro is yet to be written.

Underground Fantasies

*I*n 1880, Leadville was alive with excitement. Prosperity from the rich mines fueled the town's around-the-clock, carnival-like atmosphere. It was predicted that the area would die after the placer gold was panned out, but rich silver strikes changed all of that. In 1878, only a few hundred miners were working in the area. The population jumped to an estimated thirty thousand within two years.

A small man dressed in a typical eastern-cut suit stepped off the early morning Denver & Rio Grande train at the Leadville depot. His name was Orth Stein, and his starched collar and derby hat set him apart from the casual dress of the hundreds of people that filled Leadville's streets. Smoke from the smelters blackened the sky, and ore wagons jammed the roads down from the mines. Leadville, in 1880, was a rip-roaring town with 82 saloons, 21 gambling establishments, 35 houses of prostitution, 38 restaurants, 4 theaters, and 3 newspapers. Many of the houses of pleasure never closed their doors.

Orth Stein was a perceptive journalist hired by Carlyle Channing Davis, publisher of the Leadville *Chronicle*. Leadville was unbelievable in its violence, shootings, and bizarre behavior, but Orth Stein would surpass that reality with his own brand of imaginative fantasies.

Stein wasn't expectd to show up at the *Chronicle* office until evening, so he set out to do some sightseeing. He pushed his way through the crowds moving along Chesnut Street. As he passed down the busy street, he noticed an unusual number of doctor's offices. Curiosity prompted him to visit a few of them.

He pretended to be a medical student, and his eastern outfit made the story believable. He told the various "doctors" that he was in Leadville for some practical experience. Most of these doctors had their credentials hung unusually high on their office walls. At one office, Stein removed a "diploma" from its frame while the doctor was out. It was nothing more than a certificate from a plasterers union. Some of the so-called doctors boasted of high fees and how they practiced without a medical education.

By late afternoon, Orth had sufficient evidence for a great exposé. He wrote the story, went to the *Chronicle* office, and introduced himself to C.C. Davis. To the amazement of the publisher, who was about to give Stein his first assignment, Orth turned over the completed manuscript. Davis was so impressed that he promoted Stein from a cub reporter to city editor on the spot. The next day, the *Chronicle* ran the story on how few of Leadville's doctors were legitimate.

Given a pad of paper, Orth Stein could excite, infuriate, and insult his readers. His reporting was excellent, but this was not what made him famous. Stein generated some of the greatest tongue-in-cheek tales ever to appear in the West.

For example, in one of his articles, Orth imagined himself walking over the mountains one Sunday afternoon. He stepped on a soggy area that suddenly gave way. After slipping some distance down a forty-five degree slope, he found himself in a vast cavern with arched entrances leading into it from all sides. Connected to the cavern through these openings were many vaulted chambers.

A stream ran through the main cavern, which also contained a great deal of placer gold. Orth was not alone. Several miners were busy panning the precious metal. Exposed veins of rich ore could be seen on the cavern walls. Having not been observed, Orth tried to slip away unnoticed. He planned to stake his own claim to this rich underground property. He couldn't get back up the steep incline, however, and was forced to reveal himself to the miners. Only after Stein agreed to file a claim on behalf of the miners did they agree to show him how to get out of the cavern.

Orth Stein was a genius of the editorial hoax. To bring credibility to his stories, he used the names of real people, actual geographical features, and elaborate details. He also serialized his fantasies. The article about the cavern and the miners set the stage for a sequel, published in September 1882.

The cavern was further explored. It had great dome ceilings, stalactites, and mineralization in its walls. The side chambers were given names like Chronicle Rotunda, Bridal Veil, Serpent's Glen, and Stein Gallery. It was the kind of rich, subterranean cavern that all miners and prospectors dreamed they could find. And naturally, Stein didn't keep the place secret. In one of his imaginative articles, he "invited" fifty well-known Leadville residents to explore the cavern with him. He named it Cyclopean Cave, and as other stories appeared, new "discoveries" were made.

An underground lake was added. Stein describes it as follows:

> No current seems to disturb its placid surface; no living thing finds life within its depths; all is silent as the grave within this buried pool, where never yet a breeze had stirred a ripple or a sunbeam played.... All of the lake is not visible from any one spot. In fact, it loses itself beneath a low rocky arch into the inky darkness beyond.

Orth carried his description of Stein Gallery further into the abstract by likening it to the Vatican by moonlight. Its ceiling was fringed with white, sparkling stalactites. With little modesty, he concluded, "This apartment had been named in honor of a Leadville newspaper man."

So believable was the Cyclopean Cave, George Croffut listed it in his *Grip-Sack Guide to Colorado*. Drawings of the cave were included.

As Christmas of 1882 approached, Orth Stein was in rare form when he related a story about a particular mine. After giving it a perfectly believable location, he continued to tell how a miner struck a hard boulder imbedded in a soft limestone formation. In the boulder was a perfectly formed shoe. It appeared to be made of old, mildewed leather, but when the miner touched it, the shoe turned out to be composed of stone. The miner believed it to be a pertrified shoe from some ancient time. Every detail had been pre-served, including a repair made to the shoe. Possibly to test the gullibility of his readers, Stein wrote that the stone shoe was on display at Livezey's Fifth National Loan office in the Clarendon Hotel block. He advised his readers not to miss it. It is unknown how many went to see the fictitious shoe, nor how the management of the loan office explained that they did not have such a shoe.

Of all Stein's stories, one of the most farfetched involved a sailing ship stranded in a giant cavern fifty feet underground. He began the story with a pair of prospectors who were sinking a shaft in a desolate area near Leadville. At the depth of fifteen feet, they heard a hollow sound each time their picks struck the bottom of the shaft. The clever prospectors tied themselves with ropes and continued digging. The bottom of the shaft finally fell away leaving the men dangling by their ropes. They gazed into a room 240 feet by 180 feet. The prospectors managed to reach a ledge and then a natural stairway.

In Stein's own words:

> Down this they scrambled, impelled by curiosity and a spirit of adventure, holding their miner's lamps above their heads and soon stood upon a tolerably level sanded floor with here and there a huge crystal of quartz, while from the roof, which arched overhead at a distance of about fifty feet, enormous stalactites (were) suspended like icicles, and catching the feeble rays of light, threw them back in a myriad of rainbow hues. The cave seemed at first empty, but as their eyes gradually became accustomed to the deep gloom, the men saw in a further extremity a huge black object, which, not without some trepidation, they approached.
>
> As they neared it, to their unbounded amazement, they made out the outlines of some sort of sailing craft, but the idea of a ship fifty feet underground was so preposterous that they thought it some fantastic mess of rocks, and not until they fairly touched the timbers would they believe the evidence of their own senses. A ship it plainly was or had been, but a ship different from any that the eyes of the astonished miners had ever looked upon. It was, as nearly as they could judge, about sixty feet long by some thirty feet wide, and lay tilted forward at an angle about fifteen degrees over a rough pile of stone. The body of the craft was

built of short lengths of some dark and very porous wood, resembling our black walnut, if it could be imagined, with the grain pulled apart like a sponge or a piece of bread, and made perfectly square.

Both ends (it was evidently intended for sailing either way) were turned up like the toe of a peaked Moorish slipper. The planking was apparently double-riveted with nails of extremely hard copper, only slightly rust-eaten, and with the heads cut or filed in an octagonal shape, while along the upper edge of the ship eleven large rings of the same metal and evidently for the securing of rigging, were continued . . .

Orth continued his detailed story of the subterranean ship making it grow in the minds of his readers. The story ended as follows:

The discovery of the junk-like ship with its unknown architecture, hermetically sealed in a cavern fifty feet below the surface of the earth, gives scope to indefinite speculation. The only possible explanation seems, however, that in ages ago . . . a vessel bearing a crew of bold discoverers, tossed by the waves then receding, left it stranded there and the great continental divide, the awful unheavals and convulsions of nature, which were known so little of and can only blindly speculate on, pressed the face of the earth together and sealed it in a living grave. And this is but a groping guess, yet in what strange old seas the vessel sailed, what unknown, ancient waters pressed against its peaked prow, under what pre-historic skies it pitched, what man can tell?

The fine detail in this story gives it a certain validity. Orth Stein's fantasies didn't hurt the *Chronicle*'s circulation either. Publisher C.C. Davis allowed Stein to diverge from his normal reporting duties to write another story. After a while, the newspaper readers didn't take Stein's stories seriously, and his stories became a source of entertainment.

It must not be overlooked that Stein was also a great reporter with a natural nose for news. But it was difficult at times to separate fact from fiction. Soon after President Garfield's assassination, a quiet little women entered the newspaper office. She purchased back issues of the *Chronicle* published since the assassination. She explained that she had been in the mountains and wanted to catch up on the news. Only Orth Stein seemed interested in her, and he followed her home. He questioned her and discovered she was Mrs. Guiteau, the ex-wife of the president's assassin. She showed Stein letters written by her former husband that shed new light on the events leading to Garfield's untimely end. This information was used to produce a powerful story, which ran in July 1881. The story was of national interest and was reprinted in newspapers all over the United States. It later turned out that Mrs. Guiteau existed only in the mind of Orth Stein.

The *Chronicle* should have been only a stepping-stone in a great writing career for Orth Stein. Instead, it was the beginning and the end. Stein left Leadville in 1882 and was almost beaten to death near a Denver hotel. He never recovered fully from his injuries and later killed a man in Kansas City. His mother spent a small fortune in his defense to save him from prison. After an extended illness, Orth Stein died in 1901.

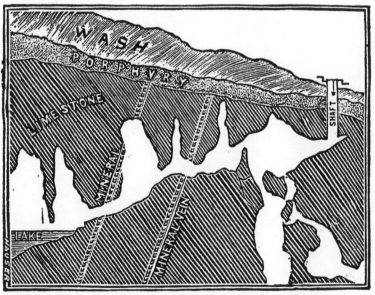

This drawing appeared in Crofutt's *Guide to Colorado* and depicts Orth Stein's imaginary Cyclopean Cave. Stein wrote many articles about fictitious places, but added almost believable realism by using actual geographical features and the names of people known to his readers.

(Denver Public Library)

Huldah's Hat

*T*he only female passenger on the stagecoach from Lake City to Denver was a Swedish girl named Huldah. The stagecoach stopped at the foot of a steep hill, and the passengers were asked to get out. This was customary on this route since the horses had difficulty getting up the hill with a full load.

As Huldah got out, her large, broadbrimmed hat sailed into the wind. It ended up on an inaccessible crag. She pleaded with the male passengers to rescue the hat, but they told her that the hat was impossible to reach. Then the Swedish girl began to cry. Her life's savings of $1,000 earned by backbreaking work doing miner's laundry was stitched into the lining. The money was saved so she and her true love, Eric, could be married after he arrived from Sweden. The men were moved by her story and managed to get the hat using the stage driver's long bullwhip.

The stage continued through the wild Colorado mountains with Huldah grateful she had her money back. At dusk, three masked men stopped the stage. The passengers were robbed of their belongings. The amount taken was not, however, enough to satisfy the robbers. They contemplated blasting open the U.S. Mail strongbox, but this would mean that every U.S. marshall in the country would be looking for them. Robbing passengers was a lot safer.

The robbers finally decided to take the risk and open the strongbox. A passenger named Bennett suddenly pointed to Huldah's hat saying, "That girl there has $1,000 sewed in her hat." The strongbox was quickly forgotten, and the robbers rode off with Huldah's hard-earned life's savings.

The other men on the coach were infuriated by Bennett's cowardly betrayal of the girl. They threatened to string him up on the spot. To save his neck, he had to promise to repay the girl all of the $1,000 when the stage arrived in Denver.

The stage arrived the following day, and the strongbox was

delivered to the U.S. Post Office. After the box was opened, Bennett produced a receipt and recovered $40,000 he had deposited in the U.S. Mail. The other men were astonished. Bennet not only paid Huldah her money, but purchased her an elaborate trousseau. The Swedish girl met her sweetheart in grand style when he arrived.

Two Funerals
for
Madam DeVere

When her business began to slow down in Denver, Pearl DeVere moved to the boomtown of Cripple Creek. She was quite wealthy and opened a parlor house on Myers Avenue in the middle of Cripple Creek's red light district. Her business prospered. Her girls were encouraged to look their best and ride around town on rented horses to more or less advertise Madam DeVere's house.

Most of the cribs on Myers Avenue were destroyed in Cripple Creek's 1896 conflagration, and among them was Pearl's place. She replaced her wood frame structure with a new, all-brick, two-story building called the Old Homestead. Her new parlor house had electric lights (instead of gas), running water, and two bathrooms. An intercom system was installed as well as a telephone (for business appointments, of course). Only the rich could afford this luxurious brothel. The bill of fare included fine food, the best liquor, and beautiful women.

One Friday night in June 1897, Pearl dressed in a pink chiffon gown imported from Paris for a party that lasted until dawn. Later Pearl was nervous and couldn't sleep. She asked one of her girls to stay with her. Around noon, the girl awoke to find Pearl DeVere breathing heavily. It was obvious the madam was seriously ill. She had taken an overdose of morphine, and she died that afternoon.

When Pearl's sister arrived for the funeral, she saw the corpse lying in a coffin at the funeral parlor. Pearl had told her family that she was in Cripple Creek designing dresses. When her sister learned what Pearl's real occupation was, she departed on the next train.

Pearl was generous and helped many a poor miner. The people of Cripple Creek were shocked by the sister's insensitivity. Funeral plans were made with the cost to be offset by auctioning Pearl's elegant Paris gown. Before the auction, an anonymous admirer donated $1,000 with instructions that Pearl was to be buried in her fine gown.

The funeral for Madam Pearl DeVere was quite an affair. The Elks Band led the procession. Pearl's body reposed in a lavender casket covered with white and red roses. Following the hearse was Pearl's single-seat phaeton with red wheels, and on its seat was a cross of pink carnations. Heavily veiled girls from the Homestead House and other establishments along Myers Avenue followed the procession in buggies up to Mount Pisgah cemetery.

This was not to be Pearl's last funeral. On July 21, 1977, Pearl DeVere was given her second funeral. A Cripple Creek resident glorified the prostitute by organizing the "Pearl DeVere Affair." Some of the events included a musical, a contest for the best eulogy, and the funeral procession itself. A wagon piled with flowers served as the hearse. Many local people, including some very attractive girls, dressed for the event in period costumes. At Pearl's grave, a eulogy was given. The "Pearl DeVere Affair" was intended to be an annual event, but has yet to be repeated.

"Billiards, Anyone?"

*J*ohn Q. A. Rollins was tall and broad. He arrived
in Denver in 1866 at a time when many who
won fortunes one day lost them the next. About two o'clock
in the afternoon, Rollins stopped at a billiard hall over
Brendlinger's cigar store at Blake and F Streets. A banker
named Charles A. Cook struck up a conversation with
Rollins. The two men talked about mining, real estate, and a
variety of subjects. Eventually, their conversation turned to
billiards. Cook, confident of his skill, laughed at Rollins when
the latter said he could beat him. Rollins challenged Cook
and gave away twenty points in each game of one hundred.
Charles Cook responded to the challenge by betting $400 on
each game. In addition, the two men agreed that they would
play until one of them gave up. At that point, the indivdual
who quit would have to forfeit $1,000.

The men shed their coats and selected their cues. Play
began at about three, and Rollins took an immediate lead
despite the twenty point handicap. Charles Cook seemed to
have unusually bad luck as the balls broke the wrong way.
He continued to play, letting nothing disturb his concen-
tration. As darkness came, lamps were lit. Amid cigar smoke,
the game continued.

Rumor of the billiard match spread through Denver, and
the hall was soon filled to capacity with spectators. Marked
with chalk, the floor served as a score pad that everyone could
see. By ten o'clock in the evening, the two antagonists were
still at it. Money was flowing steadily from Cook's pockets as
he lost game after game. At midnight, however, Rollins began
to fatigue, and the game swung in favor of Cook. As Cook
smelled revenge, he raised the stakes to $800 per game, and
Rollins agreed.

Interest in the game continued on through the night, and
Cook continued to win until an hour before dawn. Then
Rollins got his second wind, and the tide swung the other way.

Cook struggled against the odds as the chalk marks on the floor piled up against him.

The game continued on through the following day, and some merchants closed their businesses to see the match. Cook would occasionally make a brilliant shot, but the run of luck was decidedly against him. By noon, John Rollins was several thousand dollars ahead as he calculated the angle required for every shot. In contrast, Cook took what he could get and aimed for direct results.

After thirty-two hours of continuous play, the adversaries looked as pale as the tips of their cues. Their appearance clearly showed the strain on their nerves. Cook trailed by a staggering $12,000, but continued to play to win. Rollins was weary and dragged his body slowly around the billiard table after each shot. Finally, at an hour before midnight, Rollins gave up, forfeited the $1,000, and took the $11,000 Cook owed him. The players shook hands, went to bed, and never made any effort to renew the match.

John Rollins later made a fortune in gold mining in Gilpin County. He invested in a stage line, saltworks in South Park, a toll road over Rollins Pass, and founded the small town of Rollinsville. By 1879, Rollins owned 20,000 linear feet of gold-bearing veins, 300 acres of placer gold mining deposits, and 2,000 acres of farm land. Charles Cook also became a wealthy man as he continued his banking career.

John Q. A. Rollins played an incredible billiard match with Charles Cook and won $11,000 in the process. The match lasted thirty-three hours. Later in his life, Rollins made a fortune in gold mining. Rollins Pass and Rollinsville are named after this Colorado pioneer.

(Colorado Historical Society)

Trackless Train

*D*uring the winter months, the floor of South Park becomes frozen tundra. High winds, blowing snow, and sub-zero temperatures combine to obliterate the features of this high valley. Surrounded by peaks over 14,000 feet, South Park spawns some of the most severe weather conditions in the Rocky Mountains. In the summer, however, the high meadows form a lush carpet for grazing cattle. Hence, South Park supports an extensive cattle industry.

Livestock must be kept moving during the winter, and they must be fed regularly to survive. During the days when the Denver, South Park & Pacific operated its diminutive narrow gauge trains through the park, the cattle had favorite crossings. The many footfalls of the cattle would pack the snow between the rails. The snow would eventually form solid ice between the rails that could easily derail a train.

In February 1985 a long train of empty cars pulled by a small locomotive left Como for the Baldwin coal mines, north of Gunnison. The weather was very cold, and the wind whipped the snow across the bleak, rolling floor of South Park. Unexpectedly, the engineer saw an ominous shape in the distance. As the train got closer, it turned out to be a large haystack. The engineer quickly applied the brakes and brought the train to a stop. The ranchers were always doing dumb things like putting haystacks wherever it suited them, thought the engineer.

The train crew walked up from the caboose to see what the problem was. They examined the haystack in front of the engine, then looked down at the ground only to discover that there were no rails under the locomotive, or for that matter, under any portion of the train! In fact there were no rails to be seen anywhere. The train had quietly left the track at an ice-packed cattle crossing and was traveling across the frozen ground. The haystack saved the engineer from continuing across South Park without the benefit of a railroad track.

A crew member was sent back to the nearest station to get help. It was some time before the train could be towed back to the track because of the length of cable required.

The Denver, South Park & Pacific was absorbed into the Union Pacific system and was called the Denver, Leadville, & Gunnison. The U.P. went bankrupt and the narrow gauge line was taken over by the Colorado & Southern in 1898. In 1938, most of the old Denver, South Park & Pacific was scrapped.

His Head
At His Side

*P*aradox Valley is located in the remote south-western part of Colorado near the Utah border. The only community of any size in the valley is Bedrock. This area lacks the mineral wealth of the San Juan mountains to the southeast, but there have been a few copper mines there. The Cashin mine operated intermittently during the 1920s, and its owner, Mrs. Gates, employed Lemuel Hecox as her trusted watchman. He lived in the small caretaker's cabin next to the mine entrance. Locally known as "Slim," Lemuel toted a brace of big .44 caliber six guns. He claimed he was related to Wild Bill Hickock and that his name "Hecox" was nothing more than an abbreviation for "Hickock." No one took Slim seriously.

What set Slim Hecox apart from other men in Paradox Valley was the three or four thousand dollars he carried in his money belt. After a few drinks in Bedrock's only bar, Slim would freely display his fortune to any man who would look and listen to his stories. He boasted that it was his share of the loot taken from the bank in Coffeyville, Kansas, when he rode with Jesse James.

Although Slim's stories could hardly pass as the truth, the money was real. His friends advised him time after time not to show off the money belt and to find a good bank to hold his fortune. Slim's reply was always the same. He would simply pat the handles of his brace of big .44's and practically dare anyone to try to take his money. To back up his claim, Hecox would display his quick draw and accurate shooting.

Meanwhile, a band of ten men met secretly in an abandoned building in Bedrock. Late one night they plotted to drive all law-abiding citizens out of Paradox Valley by using fear and terrorism. They elected to leave an unmistakable trademark of their work. Decapitation of their victims became part of their cult. Because of the large sum of money he carried, Slim Hecox was singled out as the gang's first target.

The younger members of the gang made friends with

Hecox. A few days after Thanksgiving 1921, the young men made their way to the Cashin mine and Hecox's cabin. They knocked on the door, and Slim gladly let them in. Being caretaker at a mine was a mighty lonely life, and Slim welcomed any visitors. They all sat down at the table in the center of the room, and while they were talking, other members of the gang hid by an open window. When the time was right, one of them fired at Slim. The poor watchman died instantly as the bullet passed through his temple and lodged in the cabin wall. The gang members then lopped off the dead man's head, took the money belt and departed with the head. They rode up La Sal Creek about fifteen miles and buried the head in an irrigation ditch.

Slim's body was eventually discoverd. The only thing the sheriff could do was to direct that the body be buried in the Paradox cemetery.

One thing the gang hadn't counted on was Mrs. Gates. She hired a trio of the best detectives from Chicago to track down Slim's killers. After some work and by asking the residents of Bedrock a lot of questions, the detectives learned about the gang's meeting place. A posse was organized and hid near the abandoned building. When the gang arrived, they were arrested.

In this remote part of Colorado, the local "law" was not above using a bit of force to achieve desired results. The lonely watchman and his tall tales were dear to the hearts of those who lived in the area. Confessions were quickly extracted from the gang members, and they admitted killing, then decapitating Slim. They also told where they had buried the head. Montrose County Sheriff Dorsey, with one of the Chicago detectives, had the dubious honor of recovering it from the irrigation ditch.

The citizens of Paradox Valley felt it was only right to bury Slim's head with the rest of his body. Some thought that if they didn't, his ghost would haunt them forever. Slim's coffin was dug up and pried open. The local coffin maker had not used any more lumber than was called for. Milled lumber

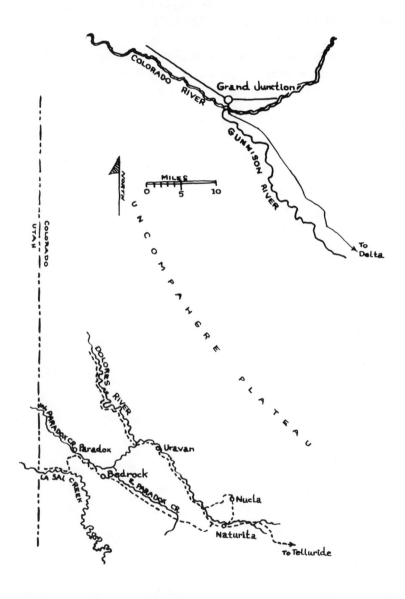

was expensive. The box was only long enough for the headlesss corpse, and there was simply no room above the shoulders for the missing part. The only choice was to tuck Slim's head inside his bent elbow.

Slim Hecox's murderers were brought to justice, and as for Slim, he rests in peace in the Paradox cemetery holding his head at his side.

KEN JESSEN

The Duel

*I*n the spring of 1878, an informant came into the office of the *Silver World* in Lake City. He approached William P. Harbottle, associate editor, and invited a representative of the paper to be present at a duel. The informant's name was Taylor, and he claimed to have been grossly insulted by "Doc" Kaye over a matter which may have involved competition for a "lady of the evening." Taylor felt that nothing short of a duel could heal the hurt he had endured. "Doc" Kaye, not an aggressive man, was of small build, and looked like he was all legs.

The scene selected for the *affaire d'honneur* was near the towering cliffs along Henson Creek just outside of Lake City. The men chose deadly shotguns. The valiant little Doc was very serious as he carefully inspected his firearm. Seconds were picked, and the code of the duel was fully explained as the combatants listened intently.

The guns were loaded with a type of ammunition not found in a gun shop or hardware store. The courageous Doc prepared himself, while Taylor was calm and dignified. Positions were taken, and onlookers fled to the safety of the nearest rocks.

The count was made and at "three," the guns barked. Echoes reverberated from the high cliffs. The little man fired first at point blank range. Taylor's shot went wide as he slumped to the ground. The gun fell from his hand, and soon the ground was reddened with his blood. Doc, horror-struck, stood for a moment, then tossed his weapon aside and fled toward Lake City. Near the old tollgate for the road up Henson Creek, Doc plunged his head into a hole. Like an ostrich, he hid his head with his body still exposed.

Taylor, the man Doc had cut down only moments before, pulled the little man out of the hole. To Doc's utter astonishment and relief, his enemy was alive and well. Taylor suggested a less violent method to settle their differences.

The crowd agreed, and the men walked off to the nearest saloon for some refreshments.

This roaring farce was carefully planned right down to the spectators. Blank shells were used in the guns, and a sponge filled with red ink provided the blood. Practically everyone but Doc was in on the hoax.

Snippy Killed by Alien Invaders

On a clear September night in 1967, a flying saucer descended in the San Luis Valley. Area residents saw the pulsating red, green, and white lights. The saucer landed on the King Ranch about twenty miles northeast of Alamosa. The aliens wanted to examine a horse named Snippy. First they slit the three-year-old gelding's throat, then they skinned the head and neck, removing the flesh down to the bone. The fiendish invaders sucked out the animal's brains and spinal fluid. Finally, they ended their bizarre ritual by removing some of the animal's organs.

The weight of their spaceship crushed a small bush. Its landing pads left a ring of indentations in the soft earth. When the ship took off, exhaust burns were left around the carcass, and a strange chemical odor permeated the air. The area was left hot with radiation. This is the story many San Luis Valley residents wanted to believe.

Mrs. Agnes King, eighty-seven years old at the time of the incident, saw the flying saucer pass over her house on the King Ranch the day of Snippy's death. Mrs. Berle Lewis, Snippy's owner, reported that a UFO landed and that its occupants killed her gelding in a most unusual fashion. "They're here," Mrs. Lewis stated, "There's no question about that. . .I know they are real, and a lot of people think I'm nuts. But if I am nuts, it is because of the flying saucers. . . I'm sure they are here. I've seen them." After Mrs. Lewis touched the remains of her horse, she experienced a burning sensation on her hands. Her boots were radioactive after she entered the area.

The Lamar *Daily News*, October 13, 1967, reported "A nuclear physicist, a psychologist, and an animal expert have been dispatched to the remote San Luis Valley, where some residents see unidentified flying objects more often than they see their neighbors."

A memorial fund was started to finance a monument to Snippy.

A plaque was to be purchased to mark the spot where the historic event took place. In addition, a fiberglass statue of Snippy was to be placed in the Alamosa city park.

Combining science and common sense, a Colorado State University professor offered a theory on how Snippy actually died. Dr. O. Robert Adams of the CSU Veterinary College examined the carcass and showed that the horse had an infection in its right flank that was probably killing it. Dr. Adams speculated that someone found the suffering horse and cut its throat to put it out of its misery. Predators cleaned the head and neck and removed the organs. In the heat of the day in the San Luis Valley, the brain and spinal fluid evaporated. The darkened "exhaust" marks around the animal were dried blood. The individual taking the geiger counter readings was not trained, the instrument was out of calibration, and radiation levels measured later were perfectly normal.

But what about the circle of indentations and the crushed bush? Robert Fenwick, a Denver *Post* columnist, advanced another theory: Snippy could have been the victim of an old-fashioned slaughter with a prankish twist. Fenwick speculated that Snippy was felled by a tranquilizer gun, then strung up, hind legs first. The horse was suspended on a pole rig resembling a tepee. This left the circle of indentations in the ground. After slashing the horse's throat, the head and neck could have been lowered into a bucket of acid. This would have removed the skin and flesh, right down to the bone. Splattered acid would account for the "exhaust" marks around the carcass. The burning sensation experienced by Mrs. Lewis could have come from the acid.

Snippy's remains lay rotting through September, October, November, and December. By that time, the carcass was pretty ripe, but Dr. Wallace Leary, operator of the Valley Veterinary Clinic, asked Mrs. Lewis if he could have Snippy's remains. Using a pickup truck, Dr. Leary moved the carcass to his clinic. He left it on his roof, hoping that additional weathering would aid in separating the rotting flesh from the bones. After two weeks, Leary ended up with the frozen horse flesh.

Using a large caldron, Leary boiled the parts of the horse and recovered the bones. During this process, he found .22 caliber bullets in the left pelvis and in the right thigh bone. Either wound could have caused the infection that probably killed Snippy.

After the bones were dry, Dr. Leary drilled and connected them with wire. A local machine shop built a platform with supporting aluminum rods. Snippy's skelton was mounted in a standing positon and placed outside a pottery shop on U.S. 285, west of Alamosa.

But UFO tales don't die easily. A year after the incident, Mrs. Lewis reconfirmed her belief that her horse was the victim of extraterrestrial beings. A student at Kearney State College in Kearney, Nebraska wrote Dr. Adams a "hate letter" after the report on how Snippy died of natural causes was published. The letter reads,

> I have been exhaustively studying the phenomena known as "flying saucers" now for five years. True there have been many false reports, but from the knowledge I now possess, I think you are being paid by the Air Force (Blue Coats) to debunk the saucer theory.
>
> My only question is this: How much are they paying you, or is there some other type of pressure they are bringing to bear.
>
> P.S. Please answer this letter because I really would like to know "the system."

Dr. Adams handled the reply to this letter in his usual professional manner and was later commended by CSU's vice-president for the excellent job he did representing the school.

An investigation team takes samples from the remains of a horse named Snippy. The flesh had been stripped from the neck and head. The team members are from left to right, Captain Dick Cable of Colorado Springs, Kenneth Steinmetz of the University of Colorado, and Herbert Roth, also of the University of Colorado. Roth was the team leader of an earlier investigation into UFOs by the National Investigations Committee on Aerial Phenomena.

*(*Pueblo *Star-Journal)*

Horsefeathers
And Applesauce

*F*rank Rice was born in 1881 and was brought up a Presbyterian. By all the rules of human behavior, he should have become a conservative member of his denomination. Instead, he evolved into one of the most extraordinary bishops in the United States.

After turning toward Methodism, Frank Rice attended Epworth University in Oklahoma City. He couldn't tolerate their rigid teachings, however, and left school to enter the loan and insurance business. This was followed by a job as a parole clerk at the Oklahoma State Penitentiary. It was here that Rice gained insight into the problems of the less fortunate.

In 1915 Rice moved to Denver and joined a local Methodist church. He headed the largest boy's Sunday school class in Denver and was also a scoutmaster. His actions seemed to follow the lines of a pious and respectable citizen, but hints to the contrary began to crop up.

While the pastor was gone, Rice suggested that the church sponsor dances for young people. The idea was novel, but shocking to the general church membership. The pastor, upon his return, threatened to resign if the congregation approved Rice's suggestion. It all boiled down to a public debate. If Rice won, dancing would be allowed, but if he lost, an offering would be made to improve public dances. After being defeated, Rice fought the decision using his position on the *Ministerial and Church Directory*. He was forced to resign.

These events drove Frank Rice to cut his ties with traditional religions, and on May 22, 1922 he filed an application to incorporate the Big Church, Inc. The platform of this church was to simplify things. Rice also believed in sticking up for the poor and thumbing his nose at the rich and powerful. The stated purpose of the Big Church was "to live successfully to meet economic and religious conditions of the age." As part of the ritual, members were encouraged to

Bishop Rice, dressed in a sackcloth and smoking a cigar, is standing with the congregation of the Liberal church in Denver. Other members of his congregation seem to be toasting the Bishop. *(Denver Public Library)*

bathe daily and drink beer, rum, brandy, whiskey, gin, ale, wine, and other "compounds which are good for health." Permission to incorporate was denied.

Frank Rice was not to be stopped. On February 23, 1923 he successfully founded the Liberal church, and its incorporation was allowed under the laws of eleven states. Frank elevated himself to bishop and carried on the work of the Liberal church for twenty-two years.

The doctrine of the Liberal church was, "We believe in the United States...Our religion is to do good." This motto was printed on the church's letterhead. Rice believed that the purpose of the Liberal church was to help people keep themselves out of trouble and to assist them in living in today's world. Bishop Rice also believed in combining science with religion and that people were meant to live by universal laws of nature and God. The first four doctrinal rules were:

1. To do good.
2. To learn how to live.
3. To seek the truth.
4. To practice the Golden Rule.

The Bible was cited as part of the church's official literature, as well as Well's *Outline of History: A Receivership for Civilization* and Ward's *How to Live*. The *Literary Digest* was used for current events, and the official newspaper of the Liberal church was the Denver *Post*.

The Liberal church was anything but a "get rich quick" scheme. Rice insisted on no dues, no fees, no collections at any service, and that attendance be at the convenience of the church members. This relegated the Liberal church to Denver's skid row, and church assets amounted to a chair, a desk, and a typewriter.

After he founded the Liberal church, Bishop Rice ran for mayor of Denver on the Independent ticket. He was defeated, but went on to run for governor on the Andy Gump ticket. The ticket was ruled out, but Rice countered with a petition signed by one hundred people that forced his name onto the ballot. After losing, he filed as a candidate for the U.S. Senate.

The board of directors had had enough of Rice's attempts to enter politics and forbade him to run for any other offices. To defy them, Rice filed as a candidate for all the offices he could, including dogcatcher.

Prohibition was a tough time for Rice, since it deprived his church of proper sacramental drink. He applied to the authorities for ten gallons of wine, stipulating that it would be used for communion. The application was denied, and Rice tried to resign as bishop. His reasoning was, "What's the use of being a bishop if you can't dabble in sacramental wine?" After his resignation was refused, he adopted Pabst's Blue Ribbon beer as the official sacramental drink, listing substitutes in case of a beer shortage.

In the entire history of Colorado, the most unusual piece of church equipment may have been the barber chair used by the Liberal church. The purpose of the chair was not entirely clear.

The congregation of the Liberal church was predominately men. The church didn't appeal to women, and to change this situation, a lottery was held. The prize was a lady's hat, but Rice failed to understand that women want to select their own hats. The lottery hat was not claimed. During another church service, a raffle was held. The down payment on a Flint automobile was the prize, but it was not obvious how any member could afford the second payment.

Bishop Rice protested against practically every formal aspect of traditional religions, and he hated memorized rituals. Rice introduced the unique practice of praying by punching the keys on an adding machine, claiming that the God of Mathematics would eventually translate their meaning!

Rice loved to speak and encouraged others to do likewise. Many of his underprivileged members were inarticulate, however. The Bishop held meetings to rectify this, but there were some rules. The first speaker had to show a certificate of dismissal from a mental institution. This was proof positive of the sanity of that member, and few other churches could boast of such a requirement for its speakers. Should a member speak too long, Rice would step up and offer him a flower. If the speaker continued, Rice would place a screen in front of him. If worst came to worst, the speaker would be bodily removed and given a glass of buttermilk to soothe his feelings.

The Liberal church claimed to have the highest percentage of ex-convicts and former inmates from mental institutions in the United States. But among its 185,000 members were Damon Runyan, Forbes Parkhill, Babe Ruth, and Colorado Governor Billy Adams. The first saint was Phineas Taylor Barnum, and William Jennings Bryan was canonized "for the impetus he gave to (the) evolutionary hypothesis."

In 1934, Bishop Frank Rice founded the Horsefeathers and Applesauce Society, Scientific. On a printed card, which members could hand out, was inscribed, "The above named charter member is hereby authorized to exhibit this membership certificate to any person for the purpose of making it more explicit and clear why said member at this time desires to say, 'No.' Rice declared that people needed help saying "No," so he formed this club, with a dollar membership, to give people something tangible to show they had the right to say it. Besides, Rice needed the money.

Because the Liberal church had also been incorporated as a university, Rice could confer any degree he pleased, with the exception of a Doctor of Medicine. Naturally, he took full advantage of this legal ability. Honors commonly granted included a C.S.M. (Common Sense Man) and a C.S.W. (Common Sense Woman). Hundreds of degrees were given away to individuals meeting no scholastic requirement. Rice claimed that his authority came from the God of Modern Science, who appeared in his office one day and told him to grant these degrees.

Robert L. Ripley, author of "Ripley's Believe it or Not," was granted the degree of Doctor of Divinity and Universal Fact Finding Doctor. A hopeless derelict was paid fifty cents to tack pictures cut from issues of *Life* magazine up on a wall. For this, the fellow was awarded the degree of Master of Arts. He had the diploma printed and mailed it to all of his friends.

Bishop Rice was a champion of Denver's poor, and is shown here conducting funeral services for "Mickey the Moocher" on August 24, 1932. Mickey lived on Market Street and was the victim of the consumption of canned heat.

(Denver Public Library)

An alcoholic on the verge of killing his wife was made a Ph.D. and given (on paper) the directorship in a corporation. He did not kill his wife and was later committed to a mental hospital.

Rice estimated that he ordained 4,300 ministers and also passed out the title of bishop to many more. There was the Bishop of Righteous Hell, Bishop of Teeth and Health, Bishop of Atheism, and last but not least, Bishop of Say It With Flowers. On the premise that ministers could beg impunity, he saved a number of Denver's bums from vagrancy charges by granting them a divinity degree.

Alferd Packer, the Colorado cannibal who was accused of eating his five companions near Lake City, died without being absolved of his sins. This worried Bishop Rice. In 1940, Rice and six companions went to Packer's grave in Littleton. The men dressed in robes to represent Packer and his companions. A white goat named Angelica was taken along as the "scapegoat" for Packer's sins. The ceremony included selected quotes from the scriptures on cannibalism.

Despite all the eccentric things Bishop Rice did, he helped many of Denver's poor. He died of a heart attack on February 26, 1945, at the age of 64. He left no money. The associate editor of the *Rocky Mountain News* praised Frank Hamilton Rice for all the good things he had done during his life and for how he set aside personal wealth to help others.

Boomerang Locomotive

Working outside the Loveland Great Western sugar factory during the "campaign" is anything but comfortable. The "campaign" to process sugar beets begins in October and typically lasts 95 to 110 days. Men and machines are exposed to the worst winter weather Colorado has to offer. At the wet hopper where the railroad cars are unloaded, spray from the hot water jets used to thaw the sugar beets combines with the steam from the factory to produce a cold, damp environment.

For many years, a small steam locomotive was used to pull two loaded cars at a time from the yards to the wet hopper. After the cars were emptied, the little engine would take the cars back to the yard and pull a second pair of loaded cars to the wet hopper. This process went on continuously day and night during the campaign.

The locomotive was called "dinky" because it was so much smaller than the cars it pulled. The dinky was operated by one man. He had to act as the engineer, the fireman, and the brakeman as well. When the coal bunker was empty, the operator filled it using a shovel. When the engine was out of water, the operator had to fill it, and when steam was low, the operator had to shovel coal into the firebox. He also had to uncouple the cars. Each time a pair of cars was moved to or from the wet hopper, the engineer had to stop the train, walk back and throw the switch leading to the yard tracks. He then had to return to the engine, reverse it, and continue. The operation of the dinky was exhausting work under poor conditions, and required a lot of walking and climbing on and off the locomotive.

Steam locomotives had a unique feature. The amount of steam released to the cylinders to propel it forward or backward was controllable using the Johnson bar. It was like a variable transmission. On steep mountain grades, engineers used the throttle and the Johnson bar to place the locomotive slightly in reverse to brake the train.

One of the dinky's operators during the early 1970s found that the Johnson bar could save a lot of walking in the cold wind. He discovered that as he approached the switch, he could place the engine slightly in reverse, but not enough to lock the wheels and stop it immediately. The inertia of the train would carry the engine forward beyond the switch. Just before the dinky reached the end of the track, the steam pressure would stop the train. As the pressure built, the train would begin to move slowly backwards.

This particular operator would set up the locomotive as he approached the switch, step off the moving train at the switch, and watch the unattended train go to the end of the track. When the wheels of the last car passed the switch, the operator would throw it and wait for his train to boomerang back. As it returned, he would step up into the cab and resume control.

To a casual observer, it would appear that the dinky was radio controlled or had been well trained to return to its master. One day, however, this clever fellow made an error in judgement. He failed to put it in reverse hard enough and sent the dinky off the end of the track and down an embankment. He was never seen again at the controls of the diminutive locomotive.

The "dinky" operated for many years at the Great Western sugar factory east of Loveland. The operator had to play many roles: engineer, fireman, and brakeman. One clever fellow discovered he could jump off the locomotive at the yard switch, wait for the train to pass, throw the switch, and have the locomotive reverse itself and push the cars back to him.

(Kenneth Jessen)

Bibliography

COLORADO'S DIAMOND FIELD

Bartlett, Richard A. *Great Surveys of the American West.*
Norman, Oklahoma: University of Oklahoma Press, 1962,
pp 197–205.

"Great Diamond Swindle." The *Rocky Mountain News,* January
27, 1875.

Wilkins, James H. ed. *The Great Diamond Hoax and Other
Stirring Incidents in the Life of Asbury Harpending.* Norman,
Oklahoma: University of Oklahoma Press, 1958, pp
145–187.

Woodward, Bruce A. *Diamonds in the Salt.* Boulder, Colorado:
Pruett Publishing Co., 1967.

LEGEND OF THE GREAT SAND DUNES

"The Disappearing Sheep of the Sand Dunes." The Alamosa
Journal, August 6, 1885. (Republished in *The San Luis Valley
Historian,* Vol. XIV, No. 2, Spring, 1982, pp 25–28.)

Trimble, Stephen A. *Great Sand Dunes.* Globe, Arizona:
Southwest Parks and Monuments Association, 1978.

QUICKSTEP REGAINS HIS JOB

"Quickstep Makes Misstep." The Denver *Republican,* January
8, 1900.

MINER'S COMPANION IS HIS VIOLIN

Bueler, Gladys R. *Colorado's Colorful Characters.* Boulder,
Colorado: Pruett Publishing Co., 1981, p 33.

Wolle, Muriel Sibell. *Stampede to Timberline*. Published by the author, 1949.

THE KIDNAPPING OF JUDGE STONE

Digerness, David S. *The Mineral Belt*, Vol. III. Silverton, Colorado: Sundance Publications, Ltd, 1982, pp 272–273.

Galbraith, Den. "Golden Leaders Planned a Train Holdup." Part XIX. The Golden *Transcript*, April 30, 1973.

Hauck, Cornelius W. "Narrow Gauge to Central and Silver Plume". *Colorado Rail Annual* No. 10. Golden, Colorado: The Colorado Railroad Museum, 1972, p 58.

Jessen, Kenneth. *Railroads of Northern Colorado*. Boulder, Colorado: Pruett Publishing Co., 1982, pp 33–34.

Poor, M.C. *Denver, South Park & Pacific*. Denver: Rocky Mountain Railroad Club, 1976, p 65.

Smiley, Jerome Constant, ed. *History of Denver with Outlines of the Early History of the Rocky Mountain Country*. Denver: *Times-Sun*, 1901, p 599.

CAPTAIN SAM HEADS TO THE PACIFIC

Bueler, Gladys R. *Colorado's Colorful Characters*. Boulder, Colorado: Pruett Publishing Co., 1981, p 45.

Eberhart, Perry. *Guide to the Colorado Ghost Towns and Mining Camps*. Denver: Sage Books, 1959, p 141.

Fiester, Mark. *Blasted Beloved Breckenridge*. Boulder, Colorado: Pruett Publishing Co., 1973, pp 80–83.

FRANK GIMLETT GUARDS THE MOUNTAINS

Eberhart, Perry. *Guide to the Colorado Ghost Towns and Mining Camps*. Denver: Sage Books, 1959, p 263.

DEPOT IS FAVORITE HAUNT

The *Rocky Mountain News,* July 7, 1957.

COLORADO'S CANNIBAL

"A Cannibal's Confession." The *Rocky Mountain News,* March 17, 1883.

"A Colorado Tragedy—the Great Trial." The Gunnison *Review-Press,* August 4, 1886.

Bates, Margaret. *A Quick History of Lake City Colorado.* Colorado Springs: Little London Press, pp 14–17.

Bueler, Gladys R. *Colorado's Colorful Characters.* Boulder, Colorado: Pruett Publishing Co., 1981, pp 60–61.

"Change in Venue." The Denver *Tribune-Republican,* July 23, 1886.

"Denver *Post* call for Mercy and Justice." The Denver *Post,* January 8, 1900.

Eberhart, Perry. *Guide to the Colorado Ghost Towns and Mining Camps.* Denver: Sage Books, 1959, pp 384–386.

"Governor Thomas tries to clear Myth." The *Silver World,* November 29, 1930.

"Guilty—to be Hanged May 19, 1883." The *Rocky Mountain News,* April 14, 1883.

"Human Skull Found One Mile from Scene." The *Rocky Mountain News,* August 18, 1875.

Kushner, Ervan F. *Alferd G. Packer—Cannibal! Victim?* Frederick, Colorado: Platte 'N Press, 1980.

"Man-eater Packer Captured." *Colorado Prospector,* Vol. 9, No. 2 (reprints of many articles relating to Alferd Packer).

"Man-eater Packer Captured." The *Rocky Mountain News,* March 13, 1883.

"Man-eater Convicted." *Colorado Prospector,* Vol. 1, No. 2, p 1 (reprints from the Gunnison *Review-Press,* August 2, 1886 and August 5, 1886).

"Parole at Last." The Denver *Post,* January 9, 1901.

Wright, Carolyn and Clarence Wright. *Tiny Hinsdale of the Silvery San Juan.* Big Mountain Press, 1964, pp 128–132.

CLOSING THE GAP

Davidson, James Dale. *An Eccentric Guide to the United States.* Berkley, California: Berkley Publishing Co., 1977, pp 363–364.

Glueck, Grace. "The Gap That Wouldn't Stay Closed." The New York *Times,* August 20, 1972.

LEADVILLE'S SHORT-LIVED PALACE

Blair, Edward. *Palace of Ice.* Leadville, Colorado: Timberline Books, 1972.

Coquoz, Rene. *King Pleasure Reigned in 1896.* Boulder, Colorado: Johnson Publishing Co., 1969.

Harvey, Mrs. James R. "The Leadville Ice Palace of 1896." *Colorado Magazine* XVII, No. 3 (May, 1940), pp 94–101.

TIME RUNS OUT

Blair, Edward. *Everybody Came to Leadville.* Leadville, Colorado: Timberline Books, 1971, pp 27–28.

Blair, Edward. *Leadville: Colorado's Magic City.* Boulder, Colorado: Pruett Publishing Co., 1980, pp 112–114.

Smith, Joseph Emerson. "Personal Recollection of Early Denver." *Colorado Magazine* XX, No. 2 (March, 1943), pp 64–65.

COLORADO'S LIGHTNING LAB

Cheney, Margaret. *Tesla—Man out of Time*. Englewood Cliffs, New Jersey: Prentice-Hall, 1981.

Hunt, Inez and Wanetta W. Draper. *Lightning in His Hand—The Life Story of Nikola Tesla*. Denver: Sage Books, 1964.

Hunt, Inez and Wanetta W. Draper. *To Colorado's Restless Ghosts*. Denver: Sage Books, 1960, pp 174–190.

THOMPSON'S TUNNEL

Wolle, Muriel Sibell. *Stampede to Timerline*. Published by the author, 1949, pp 137–138.

THE PREVARICATOR OF PIKES PEAK

Davidson, Levett Jay. "The Pikes Peak Prevaricator." *Colorado Magazine*, XX, No. 6 (November, 1943), pp 216–225.

SOAPY SMITH: CON MAN EXTRAORDINAIRE

Blair, Edward. *Everybody Came to Leadville*. Leadville, Colorado: Timberline Books, 1971, pp 29–30.

Feitz, Leland. *Soapy Smith's Creede*. Colorado Springs, Colorado: Little London Press, 1973.

Hunt, Inez and Wanetta W. Draper. *To Colorado's Restless Ghosts*. Denver: Sage Books, 1960, pp 34–40.

Smith, Joseph Emerson. "Personal Recollections of Early Denver." *Colorado Magazine*, XX, No. 2 (March, 1943), pp 60–61.

RATTLESNAKE NOT SERVED HERE

Smith, Joseph Emerson. "Personal Recollections of Early Denver." *Colorado Magazine*, XX, No. 2 (March, 1943), pp 68–69.

POTATO CLARK GETS RELIGION

Smith, Joseph Emerson. "Personal Recollections of Early Denver." *Colorado Magazine*, XX, No. 2 (March, 1943), pp 62–64.

HIGHEST FORT IN THE UNITED STATES

Fetter, Richard L. and Suzanne Fetter. *Telluride "From Pick to Powder."* Caldwell, Idaho: Caxton Printers Ltd. 1982, pp 108–117.

Scher, Zeke. "That Stormy Period when Telluride was in Rebellion." *Empire Magazine*, August 9, 1981.

Weber, Rose. *A Quick History of Telluride.* Colorado Springs, Colorado: Little London Press, pp 35–36.

THE SOLID MULDOON

"Careful Construction for a Hoax is told." The New York *Times,* Februray 7, 1878.

"Petrified Man Discovered Near Beulah." The *Colorado Weekly Chieftain,* September 20, 1877.

"Prof. Boggs Comments on Muldoon." The *Colorado Weekly Chieftain,* October 25, 1877.

"P.T. Barnum Hits Town!" The Pueblo *Daily Chieftain,* September 22, 1877.

"P.T. Barnum Offers to Purchase Muldoon." The *Colorado Daily Chieftain,* September 29, 1877.

"Sweet Land of Promise—Beulah." *Colorado Prospector,* Vol. 12, No. 8, p 1 (originally published on February 6, 1877 in The Pueblo *Daily Chieftain).*

"The Colorado Giant, The Solid Muldoon." The *Colorado Weekly Chieftain,* September 27, 1877.

Wyant, Walter. *The Colorado Giant.* Pueblo, Colorado: Beulah Historical Society, 1980.

THE HERMIT OF PAT'S HOLE

McMechen, Edgar C. "The Hermit of Pat's Hole." *Colorado Magazine,* XIX, No. 3 (May, 1942), pp 91–98.

I'LL DANCE ON YOUR GRAVE

Blair, Edward. *Everybody Came to Leadville.* Leadville, Colorado: Timberline Books, 1971, pp 17–19.

Blair, Edward. *Leadville: Colorado's Magic City.* Boulder, Colorado: Pruett Publishing Co., 1980, pp 105–122.

LA CAVERNA DEL ORO

Parris, Lloyd E. *Caves of Colorado.* Boulder, Colorado: Pruett Publishing Co., 1973, pp 24–32, 112–116.

UNDERGROUND FANTASIES

Blair, Edward. *Everybody Came to Leadville.* Leadville, Colorado: Timberline Books, 1971, pp 20–23.

Bower, Donald E. "The Fantastic World of Orth Stein." *American West,* May, 1973, pp 13–16, 61–63.

Parris, Lloyd E. *Caves of Colorado.* Boulder, Colorado: Pruett Publishing Co., 1973, pp 42–51.

HULDAH'S HAT

Bates, Margaret. *A Quick History of Lake City Colorado.* Colorado Springs, Colorado: Little London Press, p 19.

TWO FUNERALS FOR MADAME DEVERE

Blair, Kay Reynolds. *Ladies of the Lamplight.* Leadville, Colorado: Timberline Books, 1971, pp 15–17.

Clifton, Charles S. *Ghost Tales of Cripple Creek*. Colorado Springs, Colorado: Little London Press, pp 6–11.

"BILLIARDS ANYONE?"

Rollins, John Q.A., Jr. "John Q.A. Rollins, Colorado Builder." *Colorado Magazine*, XVI, No. 3 (May, 1939), pp 110–118.

TRACKLESS TRAIN

Poor, M.C. *Denver, South Park & Pacific*. Denver: Rocky Mountain Railroad Club, 1976, p 368.

HIS HEAD AT HIS SIDE

Rockwell, Wilson. *Uncompahgre Country*. Denver: Sage Books, 1965, pp 140–144.

THE DUEL

Wright, Carolyn and Clarence Wright. *Tiny Hinsdale of the Silvery San Juan*. Big Mountain Press, 1964, pp 138–139.

SNIPPY KILLED BY ALIEN INVADERS

Adams, Mrs. O.R., Collection of letters. Fort Collins, Colorado.

"Beating a Dead Horse in Flying Saucer Case?" The *Rocky Mountain News*, October 14, 1967.

Brandon, Jim. *Weird America*. New York: E.P. Dutton, 1978, pp 51–52.

"CSU Fuddy-Duddy Says Skippy Died of Earthly Infection; Mystery Ends." Loveland *Reporter-Herald*, October 16, 1967.

"Doctor Denies Mystery in Horse's Death." Chicago *Tribune*, October 14, 1967.

"Headless Horse Mystery." Denver *Post*, October 12, 1967.

Levy, Arthur. "CSU Vet Joins Investigation of Horse's Death in Alamosa." Colorado State University *Collegian*, October 13, 1967.

Nicholas, Pearl M. "Two Bullet Holes Found in Snippy's Scant Remains." Alamosa *Valley Courier*, January 26, 1968.

"No Saucers but Statue Maybe." LaJunta *Tribune Democrat*, October 14, 1967.

Osborne, Burl. "CSU Doctor Claims Snippy Died of Natural Causes." Pueblo *Chieftain*, October 14, 1967.

Scher, Zeke. "The Return of Snippy." *Empire Magazine*, January 19, 1969, pp 34–35.

"Scientist Believes Snippy Victim of Good Samaritan." Boulder *Camera*, October 13, 1967.

"Snippy's Fund Drive Nets $100 on 1st Day." Pueblo *Star Journal*, October 14, 1967.

"Snippy Shot with Bullets, Doc Declares." Colorado Springs *Gazette-Telegraph*, January 26, 1968.

"Spoilsports Converge on Scene of Snippy's Passing: Hint Horse Tale Hoax." Loveland *Reporter-Herald*, October 12, 1967.

HORSEFEATHERS AND APPLESAUCE

Hunt, Inez and Wanetta W. Draper. *To Colorado's Restless Ghosts*. Denver: Sage Books, 1960, pp 270–291.

BOOMERANG LOCOMOTIVE

Personal observations of Kenneth Jessen.

Index

About the Author

Kenneth Jessen's first book, *Railroads of Northern Colorado* (Pruett Publishing Co., Boulder, Colorado) was introduced in December of 1982. In 1984, Ken's second book, *Thompson Valley Tales* (Century One Press, Colorado Springs, Colorado), appeared. *Eccentric Colorado* is Ken's third book. Ken also writes articles for *True West, Frontier Times, Old West,* and *Colorado Country Life.* In addition to historical material, Ken has written technical articles for almost every major trade publication in the electronics industry both in the U.S. and in Europe.

Kenneth Jessen has a BSEE and an MBA from the University of Utah in Salt Lake City. He works at Hewlett-Packard's Loveland facility as a supervisor. Ken, his wife, Sonje, and their three children, Todd, Chris, and Ben, spend their time traveling and hiking in the Rocky Mountain West.